The BIG KENTUCKY REPRODUCIBLE Activity Book!

BY CAROLE MARSH

This activity book has material which correlates with
the Kentucky Core Content for Assessment

At every opportunity, we have tried to relate information to
the History and Social Science, English, Science, Math, Civics,
Economics, and Computer Technology ILS directives.

For additional information, go to our websites:
www.kentuckyexperience.com or **www.gallopade.com**.

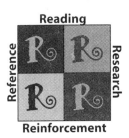

The Big Activity Book Team

Billie Walburn

Michael Marsh

Lisa Stanley

Michele Yother

Carole Marsh

Bob Longmeyer

William Nesbitt, Jr.

Kathy Zimmer

Wanda Coats

Antoinette Miller

Sherry Moss

Cecil Anderson

Chad Beard

Jackie Clayton

Terry Briggs

Jill Sanders

Cranston Davenport

Permission is hereby granted to the individual purchaser or classroom teacher to reproduce materials in this book for non-commercial individual or classroom use only.

Reproduction of these materials for an entire school or school system is strictly prohibited.

Gallopade is proud to be a member of these educational organizations and associations:

Published by

GALL**O**PADE™
INTERNATIONAL

800-536-2GET
www.gallopade.com

SHOPA MEMBER™
School, Home, & Office Products Association

NSSEA

The Kentucky Experience Series

The Kentucky Experience! Paperback Book

My First Pocket Guide to Kentucky!

The Big Kentucky Reproducible Activity Book

The Kentucky Coloring Book!

My First Book About Kentucky!

Kentucky Jeopardy: Answers & Questions About Our State

Kentucky "Jography!": A Fun Run Through Our State

The Kentucky Experience! Sticker Pack

The Kentucky Experience! Poster/Map

Discover Kentucky CD-ROM

Kentucky "GEO" Bingo Game

Kentucky "HISTO" Bingo Game

A Word From The Author

Kentucky is a very special state. Almost everything about Kentucky is interesting and fun! It has a remarkable history that helped create the great nation of America. Kentucky enjoys an amazing geography of incredible beauty and fascination. The state's people are unique and have accomplished many great things.

This Activity Book is chockful of activities to entice you to learn more about Kentucky. While completing mazes, dot-to-dots, word searches, coloring activities, word codes, and other fun-to-do activities, you'll learn about Kentucky's history, geography, people, places, animals, legends, and more.

Whether you're sitting in a classroom, stuck inside on a rainy day, or—better yet—sitting in the back seat of a car touring the wonderful state of Kentucky, my hope is that you have as much fun using this Activity Book as I did writing it.

Enjoy your Kentucky Experience—it's the trip of a lifetime!!

Carole Marsh

Color Me!

Brown
Like a Kentucky Thoroughbred
Brown

BLUE
Like the bluegrass that grows on the hills
Blue

YELLOW
Like the goldenrod
Yellow

RED
Like the Kentucky cardinal
Red

Black
BLACK
Like Kentucky coal

Purple
PURPLE
Like colors worn by a Derby Jockey

Green
GREEN
Like the Pennyroyal mint plant

Orange
ORANGE
Like a Kentucky sunset

KENTUCKY

Geographic Tools

Beside each geographical need listed, put the initials of the tool that can best help you!

(CR) Compass Rose   (LL) Longitude and Latitude
(M) Map   (G) Grid
(K)Mapkey/legend

1. _____ I need to find the geographic location of Germany.

2. _____ I need to learn where an airport is located near Lexington.

3. _____ I need to find which way is north.

4. _____ I need to chart a route from Kentucky to California.

5. _____ I need to find a small town on a map.

Match the items on the left with the items on the right.

1. Grid system   A. Map key or legend
2. Compass rose   B. Tennessee and the Ohio River
3. Longitude and latitude   C. A system of letters and numbers
4. Two of Kentucky's borders   D. Imaginary lines around the earth
5. Symbols on a map   E. Shows N, S, E, and W

Kentucky State Bird

Most states have a state bird. I think it reminds us that we should "fly high" to achieve our goals. The Kentucky state bird is the cardinal. The cardinal is a large, red, North American songbird. Cardinals have loud cheery whistles, often heard on warm mornings. The male cardinals have bright red feathers. Female cardinals are yellowish-brown with red beaks.

Connect the dots to see a cardinal. Then color the picture.

Here We Go Exploring...

Several brave men explored Kentucky in the 1600s and 1700s. Find the last names of these explorers in the word search below.

Word Bank

BOONE	WALKER	FINLEY
JOLLIET	HARROD	MARQUETTE
ARTHUR	WOOD	

```
W  A  F  T  H  A  R  R  O  D  B
O  B  X  D  F  W  G  O  A  L  O
O  S  W  F  B  T  X  H  R  S  O
D  H  U  I  R  L  E  D  T  Q  N
F  M  V  N  S  C  Y  P  H  Z  E
L  W  A  L  K  E  R  E  U  G  H
O  E  R  E  R  D  W  C  R  D  F
B  O  M  Y  J  O  L  L  I  E  T
H  X  V  Z  W  M  E  Z  B  O  J
R  W  M  A  R  Q  U  E  T  T  E
```

Local Government

Kentucky government, like our national government, is made up of three branches. Each branch has a certain job to do. Each branch also has some power over the other branches. We call this system checks and balances.

See if you can match each official with the correct branch of government.

This branch is made up of the General Assembly which has two houses, the Senate and the House of Representatives. This branch makes and repeals laws.	This branch includes the government leaders made up of the governor, as well as appointed and elected state officials. This branch makes sure that the laws are enforced.	This branch consists of the court system, which includes local, district and state courts. This branch interprets the laws.
A. Legislative Branch	**B. Executive Branch**	**C. Judicial Branch**

1. The governor _____

2. A local district representative _____

3. A member of the General Assembly _____

4. An appointed trustee of a state university _____

5. The chief justice of the State Supreme Court _____

6. The speaker of the House of Representatives _____

7. The lieutenant governor _____

8. A municipal court judge _____

9. A district attorney _____

10. A senator _____

Did you know Kentucky has 38 senators?

Yes, and we have 100 state representatives!

ANSWERS: 1. B 2. A 3. A 4. B 5. C 6. A 7. B 8. C 9. C 10. A

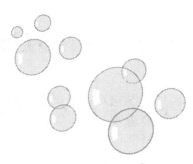

All Around
Kentucky

Bubble up on your knowledge of
Kentucky's
bordering states and bodies of water.

Fill in the bubblegram by using the clues below.

1. A state west of Kentucky
2. A state northeast of Kentucky
3. A state northwest of Kentucky
4. A state east of Kentucky
5. A state south of Kentucky
6. A river on the northern border of Kentucky

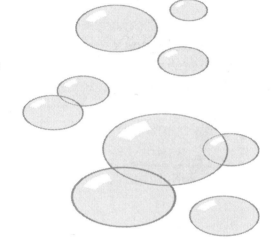

1. _ _ _ _ ⬭ _ _ _

2. _ _ _ _ _   _ _ _ _ _ _ _

3. _ _ _ _ _ _ _ _ ⬭

4. _ _ _ _ ⬭ _ _ _ _

5. _ ⬭ _ _ _ _ _ _ _

6. _ _ ⬭ _ _ _

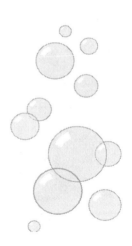

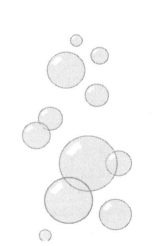

Now unscramble the "bubble" letters to discover the mystery word that answers
this question: What kind of animals are thoroughbreds?

MYSTERY WORD: ___ ___ ___ ___ ___ ___

Symbols of the United States

These are some of the symbols that remind us of America. We show these symbols honor and respect.

Color each symbol.

American Flag

Statue of Liberty

Bald Eagle

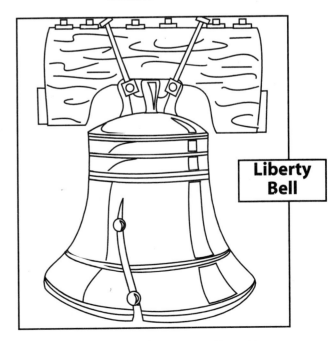

Liberty Bell

Delicious Dish

Kentuckians love a spicy stew called "burgoo."
Burgoo is a spicy stew that can be made with
chicken or beef. Lots of people like to make it
from their own special recipes.
What do you like in yours?

How many spoons are on the page?

How many forks are on the page.

How many dishes are on the page?

Color the spoons, forks, and dishes.

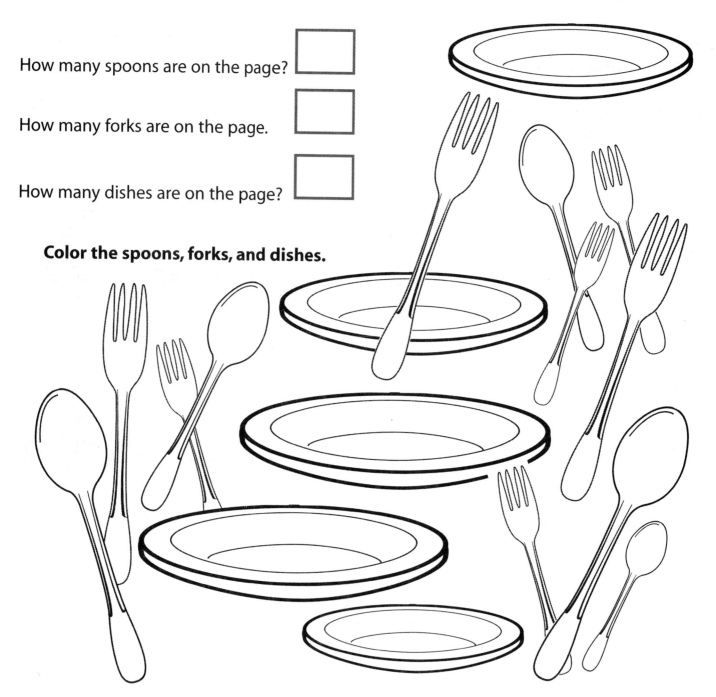

Kentucky Wheel of Fortune, Indian Style!

The names of Kentucky's many Native American Indian tribes contain enough consonants to play ... Wheel of Fortune!

See if you can figure out the Wheel of Fortune-style puzzles below! "Vanna" has given you consonants in each word to help you out!

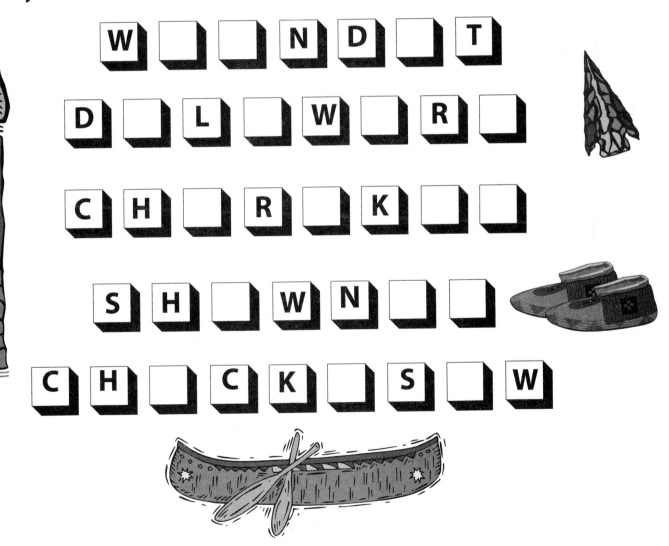

W _ _ N D _ T

D _ L _ W _ R _

C H _ R _ K _ _

S H _ W N _ _

C H _ C K _ S _ W

Bird Search!

Find the names of these Kentucky birds in the word search below.

Word Bank

CARDINAL
CATBIRD
JUNCO
WAXWING
NUTHATCH

BLUEJAY
BOBWHITE
WARBLER
OWL

```
W  A  X  W  I  N  G  L  N  Z  B  J
C  B  S  D  A  B  A  A  U  U  L  U
X  L  H  Q  R  O  U  V  T  H  U  N
W  A  R  B  L  E  R  F  H  P  E  C
L  V  F  T  E  G  A  I  A  V  J  O
F  G  B  O  B  W  H  I  T  E  A  L
M  I  S  K  O  T  O  L  C  C  Y  N
D  L  O  W  L  E  P  B  H  V  G  R
C  A  R  D  I  N  A  L  F  E  A  O
D  S  M  C  A  T  B  I  R  D  O  L
H  W  O  O  D  P  E  C  K  E  R  G
```

Rainbow, Pretty Rainbow

Rainbows often appear over the Kentucky countryside after a storm. Rainbows are formed when sunlight bends through raindrops. Big raindrops produce the brightest, most beautiful rainbows. You can see rainbows early or late on a rainy day when the sun is behind you.

Color the rainbow in the order of colors listed below, starting at the top of the rainbow.

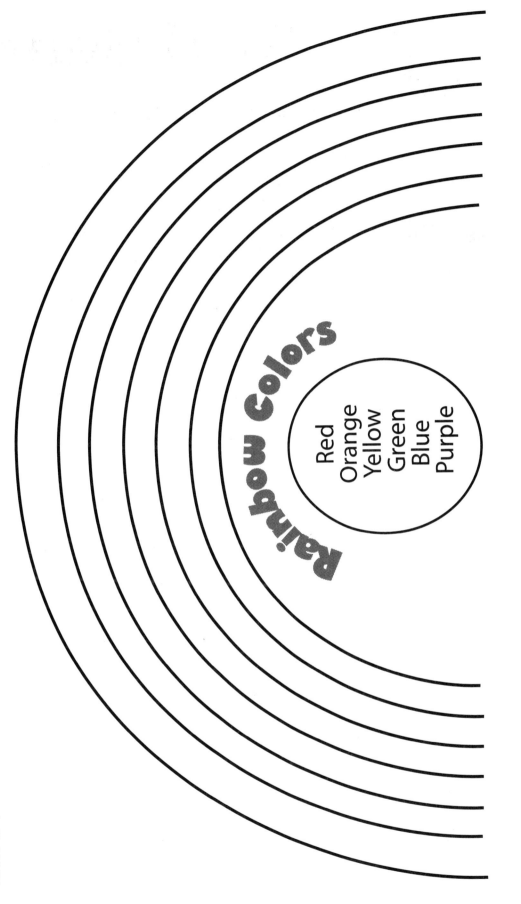

Rainbow Colors

Red
Orange
Yellow
Green
Blue
Purple

In the Beginning...
Came the French

In the late 1600s, Jacques Marquette and Louis Jolliet sailed down the Mississippi River along Kentucky's western end. Then René-Robert Cavelier, Sieur de La Salle of France followed, and claimed the entire Mississippi River Basin for France – including Kentucky!

Find your way to Jolliet.

Start
Here ↓

U.S. Time Zones

Would you believe that the contiguous United States is divided into four time zones? It is! The state of Kentucky is SPLIT between two of those time zones! That means that the eastern part of the state is in ONE time zone, and the western part of the state is in ANOTHER.

Because of the rotation of the earth, the sun travels from east to west. Whenever the sun is directly overhead, we call that time noon. But when it is noon in Louisville (Eastern Time Zone), it is only 11:00 AM in Chicago, Illinois (Central Time Zone)! There is a one-hour difference between the time zones! When it is noon in Louisville, it is also only 11:00 AM in Paducah (Central Time Zone)!
Look at the time zones on the map below, then answer the following questions:

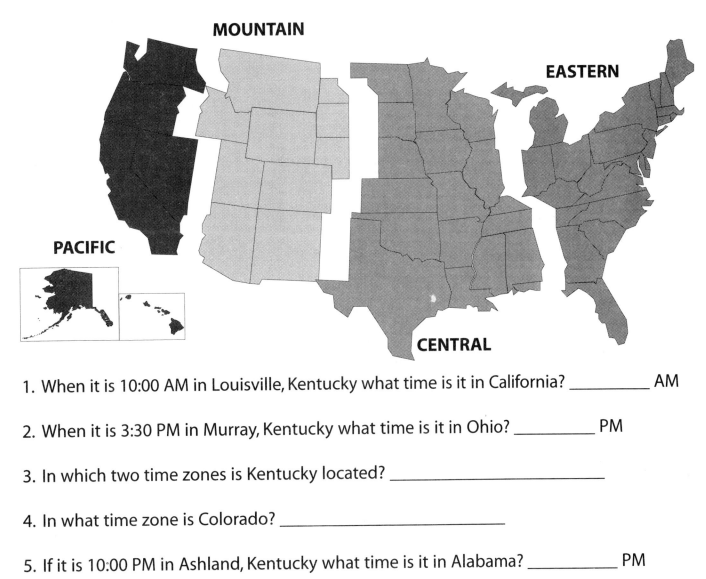

1. When it is 10:00 AM in Louisville, Kentucky what time is it in California? _____ AM

2. When it is 3:30 PM in Murray, Kentucky what time is it in Ohio? _____ PM

3. In which two time zones is Kentucky located? _____

4. In what time zone is Colorado? _____

5. If it is 10:00 PM in Ashland, Kentucky what time is it in Alabama? _____ PM

Kentucky Bird Word Jumble

Arrange the jumbled letters in the proper order for the names of birds found in Kentucky.

BLUE JAY

CARDINAL

CROW

HAWK

BROWN THRASHER

CHICKADEE

ROBIN

WILD TURKEY

WARBLER

WOODPECKER

N I D L A R A C _ _ _ _ _ _ _ _

L I D W K U T E R Y _ _ _ _ _ _ _ _ _ _ _

N I B O R _ _ _ _ _

H C N I F _ _ _ _ _

R O W C _ _ _ _

K W A H _ _ _ _

B E U L A J Y _ _ _ _ _ _ _

B R L W A R E _ _ _ _ _ _ _

N W O R B R E H S A R H T _ _ _ _ _ _ _ _ _ _ _ _

D O O W P C E E K R _ _ _ _ _ _ _ _ _

Some Patriotic Holidays

FLAG DAY

Flag Day is celebrated on June 14 to honor our flag. Our country's flag is an important symbol. It makes us proud of our country. It makes us proud to be Americans.

Count the number of stars and stripes on the flag.

_____ Stars _____ Stripes

MEMORIAL DAY

Memorial Day is also known as Decoration Day. We remember the people who died in wars and fought so that we could be free.

Circle the things you might put on a grave on Memorial Day.

VETERANS DAY

On Veterans Day we recognize Americans who served in the armed forces.

Circle ways we celebrate Veterans Day.

A State Fossil???

Did you know that Kentucky has a state fossil? It does! A Louisville classroom was asked to nominate a fossil, and they chose the brachiopod. This ancient animal can be found buried all over Kentucky. It is a mollusk (shellfish) that has two shells, or valves. In fact, it looks a lot like a clam!

Using the Word Bank, find the missing words below.

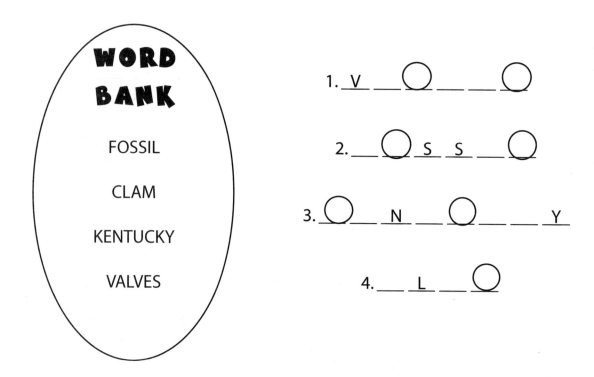

WORD BANK

FOSSIL

CLAM

KENTUCKY

VALVES

1. V __ ◯ __ __ ◯ __

2. __ ◯ S S __ ◯

3. ◯ __ N __ ◯ __ __ Y

4. __ L __ ◯

Now unscramble the "bubble" letters to discover the mystery word in the sentence below:

The brachiopod is an ancient ___ ___ ___ ___ ___ ___ ___.

Getting There From Here!

Methods of transportation have changed in Kentucky from the days of early explorers and settlers to present-day Kentucky.

Match each person to the way they would travel.

Native American

race car driver

child

colonist

astronaut

early explorer

pilot

Let's Get Geographical!

When we learn about the geography of our state, we use special words to describe it. These words describe the things that make each part of the state interesting.

See if you can match these geographical terms with their definitions!

1. gorge ___

2. canyon ___

3. tributary ___

4. region ___

5. mound ___

6. plateau ___

7. desert ___

8. mountain range ___

9. plain ___

10. highland ___

A. a sandy area with no trees or water

B. a deep, narrow passage between mountains

C. a pile or heap of earth

D. a group of mountains

E. an area of hills or mountains

F. a river or stream that flows into a larger body of water

G. an area of land

H. a deep valley with steep sides

I. an area of flat land higher than the land around it

J. a low, flat land area

ANSWERS: 1.B 2.H 3.F 4.G 5.C 6.I 7.A 8.D 9.J 10.E

Kentucky State Flag

The Kentucky state flag is blue with the Kentucky state seal in the middle. The background of the state seal is white, and the state motto is in gold. Color Kentucky's state flag.

Design your own Diamante on Kentucky!

A *diamante* is a cool diamond-shaped poem on any subject. You can write your very own diamante poem on Kentucky below by following the simple line by line directions. Give it a try!

Line 1: Write the name of your state.

Line 2: Write the names of two animals native to your state.

Line 3: Write the names of three of your state's important cities.

Line 4: Write the names of four of your state's important industries or agricultural products.

Line 5: Write the names of your state bird, the state flower, and state tree.

Line 6: Write the names of two of your state's geographical features.

Line 7: Write one word to describe your state.

The poet who didn't know it!

_____

_____   _____

_____   _____   _____

_____   _____   _____   _____

_____   _____   _____

_____   _____

_____

Kentucky,
The Bluegrass State!

Match the name of each Kentucky state symbol on the left with its picture on the right.

State Fossil

State Wild Animal

State Butterfly

State Flower

State Tree

State Fish

State Horse

State Bird

The Bald Eagle Riddle

The bald eagle is a national symbol of the United States.

Read the riddle and name each part of the bald eagle using words from the Word Bank.

1. I keep the eagle warm and dry. I am brown on the eagle's body and wings. I am white on the eagle's head and tail.
   What am I?_____

2. I help the eagle stand and wade in shallow water to catch fish as they swim past.
   What am I?_____

3. I am the eagle's home. Sometimes I measure 12 feet across.
   What am I?_____

4. I help the eagle fly high into the sky. I measure 7 to 8 feet across.
   What am I? _____

5. I am yellow. I help the eagle catch and eat fish.
   What am I?_____

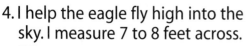

WORD BANK

nest   wings   bill
feet   feathers

ANSWERS: 1.feathers 2.feet 3.nest 4.wings 5.bill

What in the World?

A hemisphere is one-half of a sphere (globe) created by the prime meridian or equator. Every place in the world is in two hemispheres (Northern or Southern and Eastern or Western). The equator is an imaginary line that runs around the world from left to right and divides the globe into the Northern Hemisphere and Southern Hemisphere. Kentucky is in the Northern Hemisphere.

The prime meridian is an imaginary line that runs around the world from top to bottom and divides the globe into the Eastern Hemisphere and Western Hemisphere. Kentucky is in the Western Hemisphere.

Label the Eastern and Western Hemispheres.

Write PM on the prime meridian.

Color the map.

Label the Northern and Southern Hemispheres.

Write E on the equator.

Color the map.

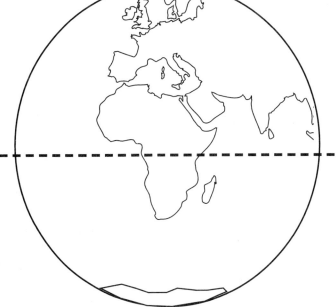

Places to go! Things to do!

Kentucky has so many cool places to go and so many cool things to do! They're located all over the state, from Louisville in the north to the Land Between the Lakes in the south.

Use the Word Bank to help you complete the sentences below and learn about some of the exciting Kentucky sites you can visit!

1. You can watch some of the most famous thoroughbred horses in the world "run for the roses" at the Kentucky Derby when you go to _____.

2. See Abraham Lincoln's birthplace and learn about our 16th president when you visit _____.

3. Every year you can ride the rides, see the animals, and play on the midway at the _____ in Louisville!

4. Cheer for the Kentucky Wildcats as they play NCAA basketball at _____ in Lexington!

5. Learn about Kentucky's history and government when you visit the Kentucky History Museum and Liberty Hall in the state capital of _____.

6. Bring your flashlight and hiking boots, and get ready to go spelunking at _____!

7. Visit the beautiful area of _____ and marvel at two huge manmade lakes, Lake Barkley and Kentucky Lake!

8. At the _____ you can take a farm tour and see more than forty breeds of horses, watch a harness maker at work, and take plenty of photos of horses!

9. See the place where Stephen Foster got his inspiration for Kentucky's state song, and maybe even see a live play at _____.

10. Visit the historic _____ to eat traditional food, see incredible handmade furniture, and watch how people lived nearly 200 years ago!

WORD BANK

Frankfort	Rupp Arena	Hodgenville
Mammoth Cave	Churchill Downs	Kentucky State Fair
Shaker Village	Kentucky Horse Park	Land Between the Lakes
	My Old Kentucky Home State Park	

ANSWERS: 1. Churchill Downs 2. Hodgenville 3. Kentucky State Fair 4. Rupp Arena 5. Frankfort 6. Mammoth Cave 7. Land Between the Lakes 8. Kentucky Horse Park 9. My Old Kentucky Home State Park 10. Shaker Village

Please Come to Kentucky!

You have a friend who lives in Arkansas. She is thinking of moving to Kentucky because she loves horses, and has heard about the Kentucky Derby and all of the horse farms in the state. You want to encourage your friend to come to Kentucky.

Write her a letter describing Kentucky and some of the things she can do with horses.

It's hard to talk about Kentucky without talking about horses! For over 200 years, horses have been a very important part of Kentucky life. When settlers first came to Kentucky, they let their horses graze in the valleys and grasslands all over the state. Horses were first used to pull wagons, carriages, and plows, but settlers liked to race their horses, too! The first Kentucky Derby was in 1875, and it's taken place every year since then!

The First Kentuckians

People have been living in Kentucky for thousands of years! Paleo-Indians lived on the land starting in 16000 B. C., and were the first to settle and hunt mastodons, mammoths, and other animals. Around 8000 B. C., the Archaic period people came to fish in the rivers. Late Prehistoric people came to Kentucky around 1750 B.C., and began to grow corn and beans. Woodland people lived in the area starting in 1000 B.C., and explored caves looking for minerals they could use to make tools or jewelry. The Mississippians also lived in Kentucky around 1300 A.D. These people built large flat-topped mounds of earth to use as temples. These mound builders mysteriously disappeared long before the land was settled by the Europeans.

Below is an empty time line. Fill in the blanks with the Native American people who lived in Kentucky at those times.

1. _____   16000 B.C.

2. _____   8000 B.C.

3. _____   1750 B.C.

4. _____   1000 B.C.

5. _____   1300 A.D.

Kentucky Rules!

Use the code to complete the sentences.

A	B	C	D	E	F	G	H	I	J	K	L	M	N	O	P	Q	R	S	T
1	2	3	4	5	6	7	8	9	10	11	12	13	14	15	16	17	18	19	20

U	V	W	X	Y	Z
21	22	23	24	25	26

1. State rules are called ___ ___ ___ ___.
12   1   23   19

2. Laws are made in our state ___ ___ ___ ___ ___ ___ ___.
3   1   16   9   20   15   12

3. The leader of our state is the ___ ___ ___ ___ ___ ___ ___ ___.
7   15   22   5   18   14   15   18

4. We live in the state of ___ ___ ___ ___ ___ ___ ___ ___.
11   5   14   20   21   3   11   25

5. The capital of our state is ___ ___ ___ ___ ___ ___ ___ ___ ___.
6   18   1   14   11   6   15   18   20

ANSWERS: 1. LAWS 2. CAPITOL 3. GOVERNOR 4. KENTUCKY 5. FRANKFORT

A Rough Row to Hoe!

The people who first came to Kentucky were faced with a lot of hard work to survive in their new home. **Circle the things settlers in Kentucky would need.**

Buzzing Around Kentucky!

Find the answers to the questions in the maze. Write them on the lines. Follow a path through the maze in the same order as your answers to get the bee to the beehive.

1. Kentucky is in the drainage basin of the _____ River.

2. Kentucky's state song is called "My Old Kentucky _____."

3. Kentucky's nickname is the "_____ State."

4. American _____ were the first people to live in Kentucky.

5. The capital of Kentucky is _____.

6. The world headquarters for Kentucky Fried _____ is in Kentucky.

7. Kentucky was founded by John _____.

8. Every year, Churchill Downs is the home of the Kentucky _____.

9. President Abraham _____ was born in Kentucky in 1809.

10. The 101st Airborne Division is located at Fort _____, Kentucky.

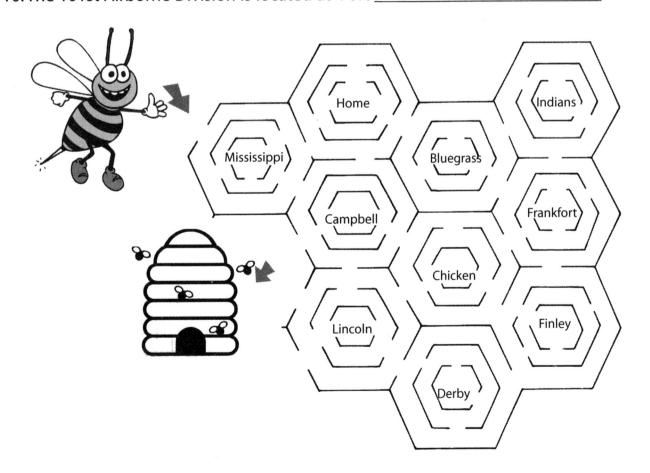

Kentucky Through the Times

Many great things have happened in Kentucky throughout its history, both past and present. **Chronicle the following important Kentucky events by solving math problems to find out the years in which they happened.**

1.	René-Robert Cavelier, Sieur de La Salle, claims the Mississippi Basin for France.	6-5=	3X2=	2X4=	8÷4=
2.	Harrodstown is founded.	3-2=	5+2=	7X1=	12÷3=
3.	Kentucky becomes the 15th state.	4÷4=	14÷2=	3X3=	8-6=
4.	Abraham Lincoln is born.	2-1=	5+3=	9-9=	18÷2=
5.	Kentucky declares it is neutral at the beginning of the Civil War.	8-7=	4X2=	12÷2=	4-3=
6.	The first Kentucky Derby is run.	5÷5=	3+5=	6+1=	10-5=
7.	The Black Patch War begins.	8-7=	3X3=	9-9=	7-1=
8.	The U.S. Treasury sets up a gold vault at Fort Knox.	4-3=	2+7=	6÷2=	2X3=
9.	The University of Kentucky first accepts black students.	0+1=	18÷2=	2X2=	2+6=
10.	The Civil Rights Act is passed in Kentucky.	8-7=	6+3=	3X2=	1+5=

ANSWERS: 1. 1682 2. 1774 3. 1792 4. 1809 5. 1861 6. 1875 7. 1906 8. 1936 9. 1948 10. 1966

Meet Joe Black!

Joe Black is a coal miner in eastern Kentucky. He is strong and works hard. He works in a coal mine and uses many tools to do his job. One is a pick, another is a shovel. Did you know that Kentucky is one of the top three coal producers in the United States? Coal is Kentucky's most important mineral product.

Joe is on his way home after working all day, but, whoops, he forgot his tools. Help Joe get back to the quarry to find his missing pick and shovel, and then go home.

Go mining for the other Kentucky minerals buried in the coal mine by accident. Circle them when you strike it rich!

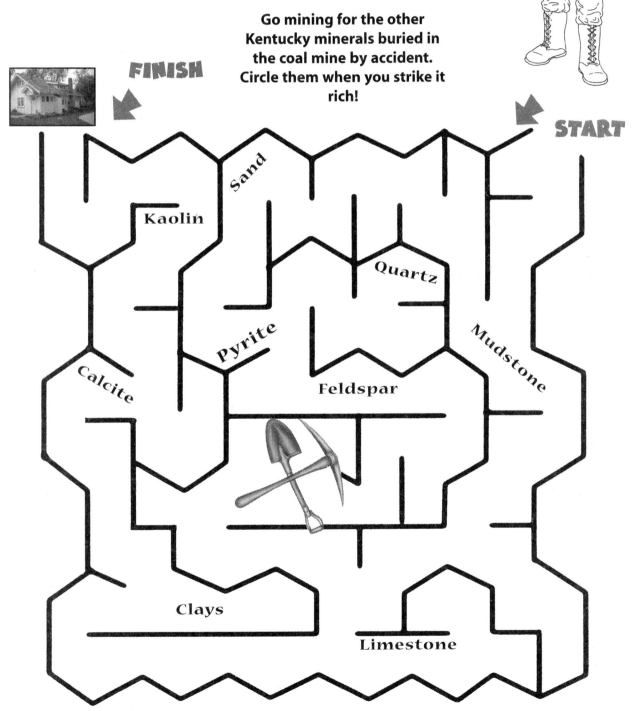

African Slaves Come to Kentucky

By 1850, almost 1 in 4 Kentucky residents were slaves. Many of the Kentuckians claimed they treated their slaves "like family." But slaves' lives were hard. The most famous slave revolt happened in Kentucky in 1848, when 55 slaves tried to escape at once. Many men, including Cassius Marcellus Clay, spoke out against slavery. Many slaves left Kentucky to fight for the North during the Civil War. Slavery continued in Kentucky until the 13th Amendment to the Constitution freed all of America's slaves.

Locate Africa on the map·························Write an "S" for Slaves.
Locate the United States on the map·········Write an "L" for Labor.
Locate the Atlantic Ocean·······················Write an "A" on the Atlantic Ocean.
Draw a line from Africa to Kentucky ···········Write a "V" for voyage.
Locate Kentucky on the map······················Write an "E" for economic expansion.

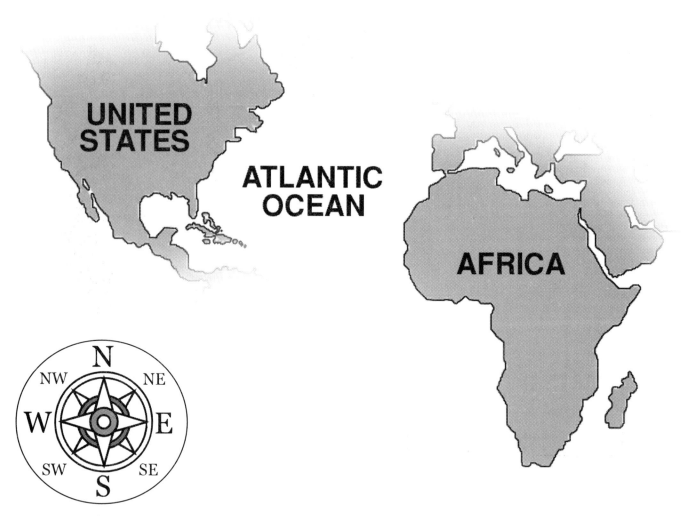

UNITED STATES

ATLANTIC OCEAN

AFRICA

N
NW   NE
W   E
SW   SE
S

What Did We Do Before Money?

In early America, there were no banks. However, people still wanted to barter, trade, or otherwise "purchase" goods from each other. Wampum, made of shells, bone, or stones, was often swapped for goods. Indians, especially, used wampum for "money." The barter system was when people swapped goods or services. "I'll give you a chicken." "I'll bake you some bread." Later, banks came into existence, and people began to use money to buy goods. However, they also still bartered when they had no money to spend.

Number in order, which items early Americans used to purchase goods and services.

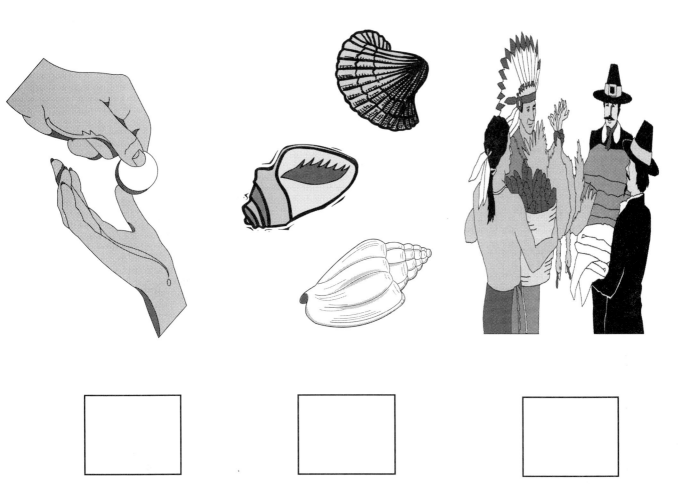

Rhymin' Riddles

1. I am a "border state," and my name starts with a "K";
   Here the Derby is run, every year the same day.

   What am I? _____

2. We hunted in Kentucky before the pioneers came;
   From that land we took fish, vegetables, and game.

   Who are we? _____

3. I was from France, and down the Mississippi I did explore;
   The land of Kentucky I claimed for France, and more.

   Who am I? _____

4. A pass through the Appalachian Mountains am I;
   A gateway to the West I became by and by.

   What am I? _____

5. I was born in this state and 16th president I became;
   From a little log cabin I went to fortune and fame.

   Who am I? _____

Map Symbols

Make up symbols for these items and draw them in the space provided on right.

coal	
horses	
lakes	
mountains	
chickens	
airport	
fort	
railroad	
hospital	

A Kentucky Basketful

Match the name of each crop or product from Kentucky with that item.

1.Coal   2.Cotton   3.Wheat   4.Apples   5.Corn

___

___

___

___

___

Kentucky's Venomous Snakes!

Three types of venomous (poisonous) snakes live in Kentucky.
Using the alphabetical code, see if you can find out their names.

A 1 B 2 C 3 D 4 E 5 F 6 G 7 H 8 I 9 J 10 K 11 L 12 M 13 N 14 O 15 P 16 Q 17 R 18 S 19 T 20

U 21 V 22 W 23 X 24 Y 25 Z 26

— — — — — —   — — — — — — — — — —
20 9 13 2 5 18   18 1 20 20 12 5 19 14 1 11 5

— — — — — — — — — —
3 15 20 20 15 14 13 15 21 20 8

— — — — — — — — — —
3 15 16 16 5 18 8 5 1 4

Battledore Goes Into Battle!

"Hi, my name is Battledore. This is my dog, Tin Whistle. We are soldiers in the Civil War. We are fighting for the Confederate Army. I am from Kentucky. So is Tin Whistle. I don't know what war is all about yet. I thought I wanted to fight, but now I'm not so sure. I'm homesick. Tonight I will sleep in a tent outside a town called Perryville. Tomorrow, I will fight in my first battle. I am excited and afraid. Wish me luck!"

Draw Battledore's tent below. Put a stack of cannonballs beside it. Also draw a campfire with a pot of beans simmering on it. Help him get ready for the big battle at Perryville.

The Battle of Perryville was Kentucky's deadliest battle of the Civil War. Union and Confederate forces met almost by accident when they both were looking for water. Neither side won, but the Confederate soldiers were forced to retreat. You can visit the Perryville Battlefield State Historic Site to learn more.

Make a Wampum Necklace!

Kentucky Indians used wampum (beads made from colored shells and stones) to barter with early settlers. They traded wampum for food and supplies. The Indians sometimes traded wampum for trinkets.

You can make your own wampum necklace using dried macaroni and string. Thread the dried macaroni onto a long piece of string and tie.

Wear your necklace to show pride in Kentucky's first inhabitants!

Using markers or crayons, color the wampum necklace.

Color the shells.

Producers and Consumers

Producers (sellers) make goods or provide services. Ralph, a 4th grade student in Louisville, is a consumer because he wants to buy a new wheel for his bicycle.

Help Ralph locate the bicycle-wheel seller so he can fix his bike!

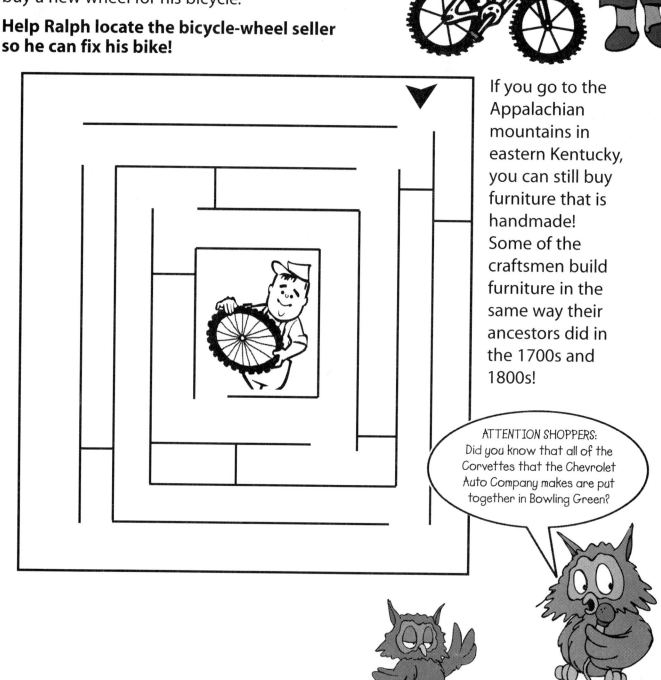

If you go to the Appalachian mountains in eastern Kentucky, you can still buy furniture that is handmade! Some of the craftsmen build furniture in the same way their ancestors did in the 1700s and 1800s!

ATTENTION SHOPPERS: Did you know that all of the Corvettes that the Chevrolet Auto Company makes are put together in Bowling Green?

Extreme Kentucky Word Wheel!

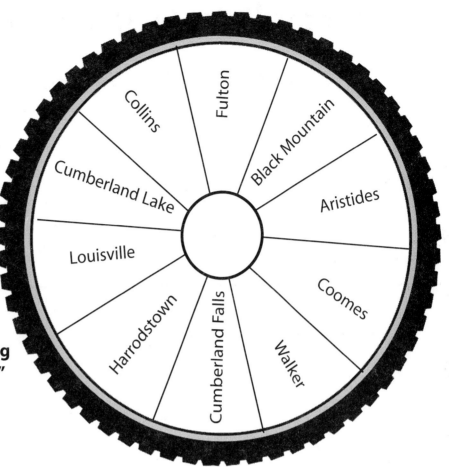

Using the Word Wheel of Kentucky names, answer the following questions about "extreme" Kentucky.

1. The highest point in Kentucky is the _____.

2. The lowest point in Kentucky can be found in _____ County.

3. Kentucky's largest waterfall is _____.

4. The largest city in Kentucky is _____.

5. The first town in Kentucky was _____.

6. The largest lake in Kentucky is _____.

7. The first school was founded in 1775 by Mrs. William _____.

8. The first man to travel through the Cumberland Gap was Thomas _____.

9. The first female governor of Kentucky was Martha Layne _____.

10. The first winner of the Kentucky Derby was a horse named _____.

"Made in Kentucky"

You might be surprised to learn how many things are grown, manufactured, or mined in Kentucky! Find the items in the word search below:

Word Bank

TOBACCO	MILK	CHEMICAL
COAL	SOYBEANS	CORVETTES
BOURBON	POPCORN	OIL

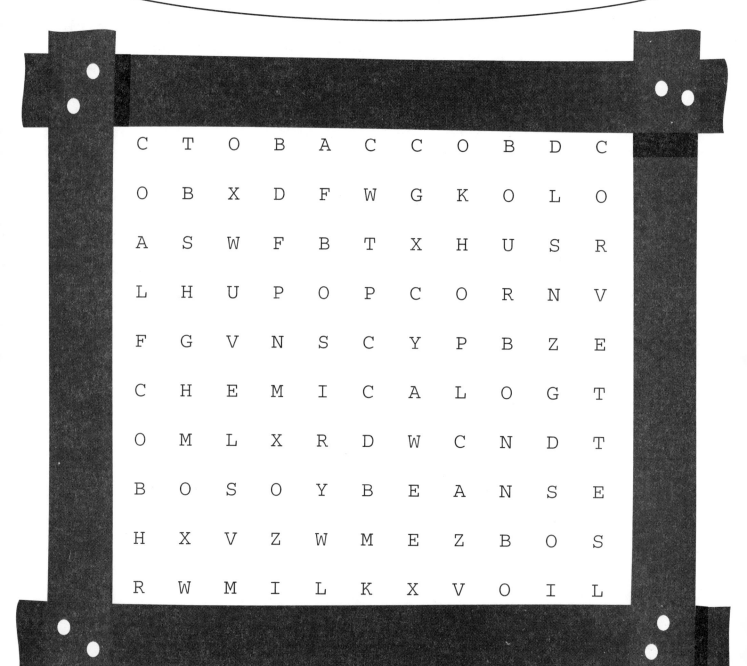

C T O B A C C O B D C
O B X D F W G K O L O
A S W F B T X H U S R
L H U P O P C O R N V
F G V N S C Y P B Z E
C H E M I C A L O G T
O M L X R D W C N D T
B O S O Y B E A N S E
H X V Z W M E Z B O S
R W M I L K X V O I L

Mixed—Up States!

Color, cut out, and paste each of Kentucky's seven neighbors on the map of the central states.

Be sure and match the state shapes!

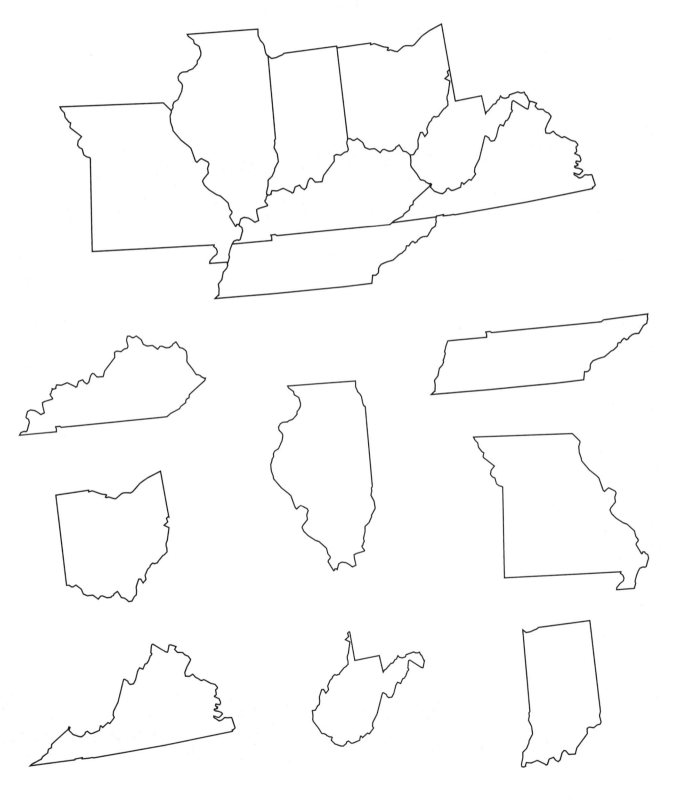

Kentucky Law Comes In Many Flavors!

Here is a matching activity for you to see just a few of the many kinds of law it takes to run our state. See how well you do!

If I am this, I might use what type of law?

1. Bank robber
2. Business person
3. State park
4. Kentucky
5. Hospital
6. Real estate agent
7. Corporation
8. Ship owner
9. Diplomat
10. Soldier

Laws of many types:

A. Military Law
B. International Law
C. Constitutional Law
D. Medical Law
E. Maritime Law
F. Commercial Law
G. Criminal Law
H. Property Law
I. Antitrust Law
J. Environmental Law

ANSWERS: 1.G 2.F 3.J 4.C 5.D 6.H 7.I 8.E 9.B 10.A

People and Their Jobs!

Can you identify these people and their jobs?

Put an A by the person working on a Kentucky farm.
Put a B by the person working as a Kentucky artist.
Put a C by the Kentucky volunteer fireman.
Put a D by the Kentucky postal worker.
Put an E by the person working for a high-tech computer company in Louisville.

Two Make One

Many Kentucky places have interesting names. Some of them are even compound words.
See if you can figure out the two words that are put together to make these place names. Write the two words on the lines below the big one.

BATTLEGROUND	ELKHORN	TEARCOAT
_____ _____	_____ _____	_____ _____
ILLWELL	LONESOME	NONESUCH
_____ _____	_____ _____	_____ _____
TORCHLIGHT	ASHLAND	NEEDMORE
_____ _____	_____ _____	_____ _____
LICKSKILLET	TIDALWAVE	TROUBLESOME
_____ _____	_____ _____	_____ _____
FOURMILE	BEARWALLOW	GEORGETOWN
_____ _____	_____ _____	_____ _____
ELIZABETHTOWN	CUTSHIN	DEADMAN
_____ _____	_____ _____	_____ _____

Politics As Usual

Our elected government officials decide how much money is going to be spent on schools, roads, public parks, and libraries. It's very important for the citizens of the state to understand what's going on in their government and how it will affect them. Below are some political words that are often used when talking about government.

MATCH THESE POLITICAL WORDS WITH THEIR DEFINITION.

1. Constitution _____

2. Governor _____

3. Chief Justice _____

4. General Assembly _____

5. District _____

6. Amendment _____

7. Term _____

8. Election _____

9. Veto _____

10. Bill _____

A. A period of years that an elected official is allowed to serve

B. Lead Judge on the State Supreme Court

C. The chief executive cannot serve more than two consecutive terms

D. An addition to the Constitution

E. The selection, by vote, of a candidate for office

F. Kentucky's law-making body, made up of the House of Representatives and the Senate

G. Written in 1777, this document established Kentucky's state laws

H. The ability to block or deny a bill or law from being passed

I. Draft of a law presented for review

J. A division of a state for the purpose of electing a representative from that division

ANSWERS: 1.G 2.C 3.B 4.F 5.J 6.D 7.A 8.E 9.H 10.I

What Shall I Be When I Grow Up?

Here are just a few of the jobs that kept early Kentuckians busy.

Lawyer	Tenant Farmer	Woodcarver
Judge	Housekeeper	Silversmith
Politician	Dairyman	Wheelwright
Teacher	Servant	Cabinetmaker
Mayor	Plantation Owner	Cooper (barrelmaker)
Carpenter	Weaver	Barber
Gardener	Mantuamaker (dressmaker)	Printer
Cook	Musician	Bookbinder
Laundress	Jeweler	Innkeeper
Stablehand	Tailor	Minister
Baker	Pharmacist	Gaoler (jailer)
Fisherman	Doctor	Governor
Prospector	Milliner (hatmaker)	Soldier
Hunter	Blacksmith	Gunsmith

You are a young pioneer trying to decide what you want to be when you grow up.

Choose a career and next to it write a description of what you think you would do each day as a:

Write your career choice here!
_____   _____
                           _____
                           _____

Write your career choice here!
_____   _____
                           _____
                           _____

Write your career choice here!
_____   _____
                           _____
                           _____

Write your career choice here!
_____   _____
                           _____
                           _____

Naturally Resourceful

Kentucky is resource-full! Full of natural resources, that is! How are these natural resources used? Write one or more ways you or your parents might use each of these resources.

Coal _____

Cattle _____

Corn _____

Cotton _____

Poultry _____

Oil _____

Our State's Governor

The governor is our state's leader.
Do some research to complete this biography of the governor.

Governor's Name:

_____

Paste a picture of the governor here: ➤

The governor was born in this state:

_____

The governor was born on this date:

_____ .

Members of the governor's family:

_____

_____

Interesting facts about the governor :

_____

_____

_____

_____

_____

_____

_____

Kentucky Indians!

Cherokee, Chickasaw, Delaware, Shawnee, and Wyandot Indians were the first people living in Kentucky. They lived in the New World before the explorers and settlers came.

Circle the things that Indians might have used in their everyday life.

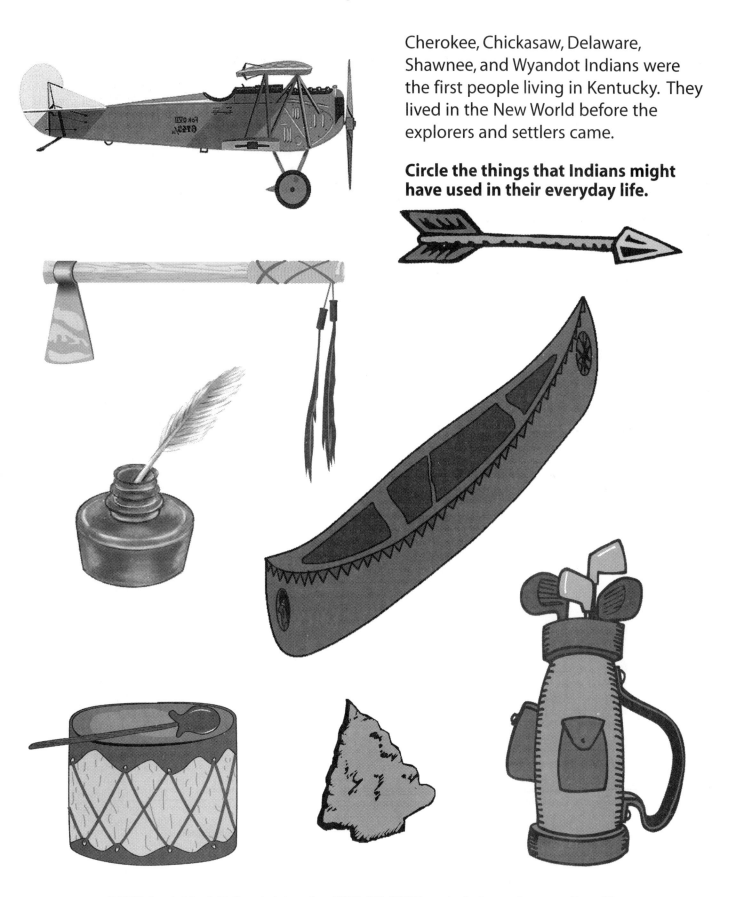

States All Around!
Code-Buster

Decipher the code and write in the names of these states that border Kentucky.

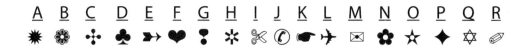

The First Americans

When European explorers first arrived in America, they found many American Indian tribes living here.

Shawnee Indians lived in the Eastern Woodland region of the United States, including Kentucky. The types of homes they lived in were wigwams.
Color the Eastern Woodland green.

Plains Indians lived all over the Great Plains region of North America. Some Plains Indians lived in teepees.
Color the Great Plains yellow.

Pueblo Indians lived in the Southwest region of North America. They lived in multi-story terraced buildings, called pueblos. **Color the Southwest red.**

Color these Indian dwellings.
Then draw a line from the type of house to the correct region.

Looking For a Home!

Draw a line from the things on the left to their homes on the right!

1. Kentucky's governor

2. Bats and blind beetles

3. Horse racing fan

4. Rare birds

5. Gold bars

6. Thoroughbred horse

7. University of Kentucky Wildcat

8. The first bluegrass singers

9. Tourist with a camera who enjoys visiting historic Civil War sites

10. Corvette looking for spare parts

A. Mammoth Cave

B. Kentucky Horse Park

C. Frankfort

D. Rupp Arena in Lexington

E. Perryville Battlefield State Historic Site

F. Bowling Green

G. Fort Knox

H. Appalachian Mountains

I. Churchill Downs

J. John James Audubon State Park

Uncle Tom's Cabin

When Harriet Beecher Stowe visited friends in Kentucky, she witnessed a terrible event. She saw a slave auction on the courthouse steps, and watched as families were torn apart. Harriet felt great anger and sadness when she saw this, and decided to write about it. In 1852, Harriet published the novel *Uncle Tom's Cabin*. Her book inspired so much antislavery feeling that many Southern states did not allow people to have it in their homes.

Imagine that you are Harriet Beecher Stowe, watching the slave auction.
Write a letter home to your family describing what you saw and how you felt.

Something Fishy Here!

All of the big lakes in Kentucky are actually man-made! Dams were built across rivers to create lakes like Kentucky Lake, Lake Barkley, and Nolin Lake. But you can be sure that the fish probably don't know the difference!

Color what is going on above the water line (a boat, fishermen, etc.) and add some other underwater fish friends.

The Scenic Route

Imagine that you are the official tour guide for your class and you're taking them on a trip to some famous Kentucky places. Watch out for the runaway horses!

Circle these sites and cities on the map below. Number them in the order you would visit them if you were traveling east to west through the state:

____ Louisville   ____ Lexington   ____ Big Sandy River

____ Black Gnat   ____ Frankfort   ____ Hopkinsville

____ Bowling Green   ____ Fort Knox   ____ Monkey's Eyebrow

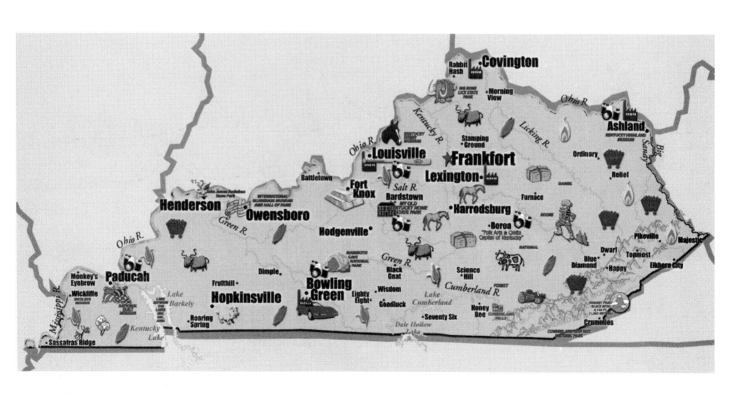

Key to a Map!

A map key, also called a map legend, shows symbols which represent different things on a map.

Match each word with a symbol for things found in the state of Kentucky.

airport

church

mountains

railroad

river

road

school

state capital

battle site

bird sanctuary

Brother, Can You Spare a Dime?

After the collapse of the stock market on Wall Street in 1929, the state of Kentucky, along with the rest of the nation, plunged headfirst into the Great Depression. It was the worst economic crisis America had ever known. Banks closed and businesses crashed...there was financial ruin everywhere. In Kentucky alone, almost half of all workers lost their jobs.

Our President Helps.

While the nation was in the midst of the Depression, Franklin Delano Roosevelt became president. With America on the brink of economic devastation, the federal government stepped forward and hired unemployed people to build parks, bridges, and roads. With this help, and other government assistance, the country began to slowly, but painfully, pull out of the Great Depression. Within the first 100 days of his office, Roosevelt enacted a number of policies to help minimize the suffering of the nation's many unemployed workers. These programs were known as the NEW DEAL. The jobs helped families support themselves and improved the country's infrastructure.

Put an X next to the jobs that were part of Roosevelt's New Deal.

1. computer programmer _____

2. bridge builder _____

3. fashion model _____

4. park builder _____

5. interior designer _____

6. hospital builder _____

7. school builder _____

8. website designer _____

ANSWERS: 2, 4, 6, 7

Kentucky Battlefields

Many Civil War battles were fought on Kentucky's soil. The Civil War ended in 1865 when Confederate General Robert E. Lee surrendered to Union General Ulysses S. Grant at the Appomattox Court House in Virginia.

Draw a line from the name of the location in which each battle occurred to its correct place on the map.

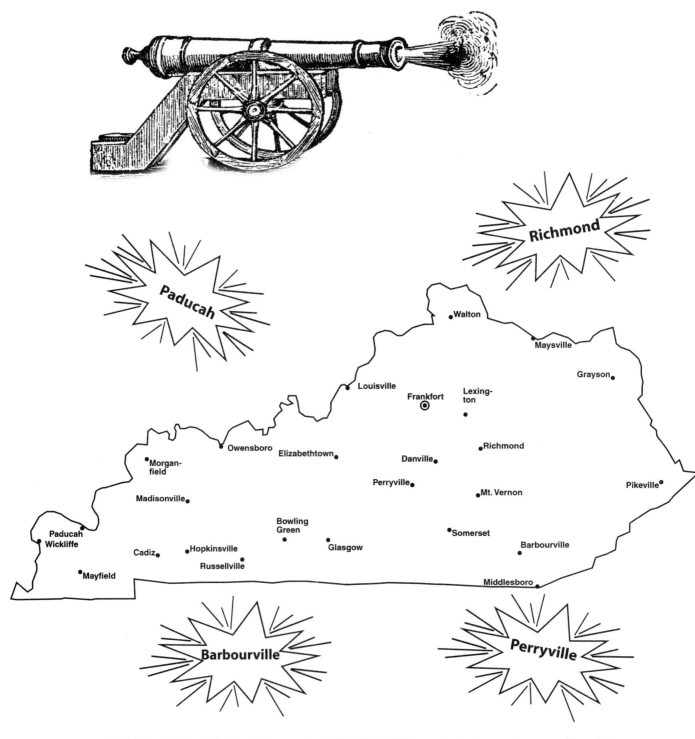

Kentucky Immigration

People have come to Kentucky from many other states and countries. As time has gone by, Kentucky's population has grown more diverse. This means that people of different races and from different cultures and ethnic backgrounds have moved to Kentucky.

In the past, many immigrants came to Kentucky from England, Scotland, Ireland, France, Germany, and other European countries. Slaves migrated (involuntarily) from Africa. More recently, people have migrated to Kentucky from South American and Asian countries. Only a certain number of immigrants are allowed to move to America each year. Many of these immigrants eventually become U.S. citizens.

Read the statement and decide if it's fact or opinion.
Write your answer on the line.

1. Many of Kentucky's early immigrants came from Europe. _____

2. Lots of immigrants speak a language other than English. _____

3. The clothing immigrants wear is very interesting. _____

4. Immigrants from England have a neat accent when
   they speak. _____

5. Many immigrants will become United States citizens. _____

6. Immigrants love Kentucky's southern cooking. _____

An immigrant is a person who migrates to another country in hopes of a better life.

ANSWERS: 1. Fact 2. Fact 3. Opinion 4. Opinion 5. Fact 6. Opinion

A Day in the Life of a Pioneer!

Pretend you are a pioneer in the days of early Kentucky.
You keep a diary of what you do each day.
**Write in the "diary" what you might have done
on a long, hot summer day in July, 1792.**

_____

_____

_____

_____

_____

_____

_____

_____

_____

_____

_____

_____

This Old House!

Take yourself back 100 years. Can you imagine what life would be like in the Victorian Era? What did turn-of-the-century Kentuckians have? How did they live? See if you can pick out which of the following items people at the turn of the century used in their homes!

Circle the things you might find or use around your 1900 home.

ANSWERS: 1 2 3 4 6 7 9 10 11 13 15 16 17 18 19 20 22

Home Sweet Home

Match these famous Kentucky authors and artists with their native or adopted hometowns.

A = Guthrie; B = Louisville; C = Henderson; D = Lexington; E = Rosine;
F = Paducah; G = Winchester; H = Bowling Green

_____ 1. **John James Audubon:** artist who is famous for his book *Birds of North America*

_____ 2. **Henry Faulkner**: artist who is famous for his paintings of animals and landscapes

_____ 3. **William Smith "Bill" Monroe**: the "father of bluegrass music"

_____ 4. **Robert Penn Warren**: Pulitzer prize winning author of *All the King's Men*

_____ 5. **Irvin S. Cobb**: journalist, humorist, and short story writer

_____ 6. **Allen Tate**: novelist who wrote *Ode to the Confederate Dead*

_____ 7. **Hunter Thompson**: author of *Fear and Loathing in Las Vegas*

_____ 8. **Duncan Hines**: food critic and author of restaurant guides

ANSWERS: 1.C 2.D 3.E 4.A 5.F 6.G 7.B 8.H

Weather to Please!

Kentucky's weather can range from hot and humid summers to typically mild winters. The highest temperature ever recorded was 114º F (46º C) in 1930, but a typical July will range from 66º F (19º C) to about 87º F (31º C). In the southern and western parts of the state, summers can be exceptionally warm.

The coldest Kentucky temperature was recorded in 1963, when it dropped to -34º F (-37º C)! Usually, winter temperatures in January are between 23º F (-5º C) and 43º F(6º C). Temperatures can drop below freezing, but these cold periods don't last very long.

One thing Kentucky gets plenty of is RAIN! It usually gets an average of 47 inches (119 centimeters) of precipitation a year. That includes both rain and melted snow! All this water is one of the reasons that Kentucky has so many rivers, creeks, swamps, and ponds.

On the thermometer gauges below, color the mercury red to show the hottest temperature (ºF) ever recorded in Kentucky. Color the mercury blue to show the coldest temperature (ºF) ever recorded in Kentucky.

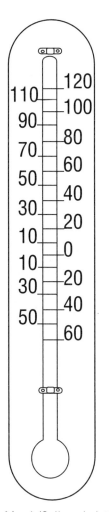
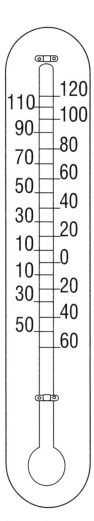

Kentucky Women and the Vote

Before women were able to vote, Madeline Breckinridge was a crusader for women's rights. She was the great-granddaughter of Henry Clay. Madeline said that politicians would listen to women only when women could vote. In 1920, enough states ratified the 19th Amendment to the Constitution, and it became the law of the land. Women gained suffrage nationally and began voting in Kentucky for the first time. Women today continue to be a major force in the election process.

Match the words on the left with their definitions on the right.

1. Amendment _____

2. Ratify _____

3. Constitution _____

4. General Assembly _____

5. Law of the Land _____

6. Election _____

7. Suffrage _____

8. Women _____

a. The right to vote

b. A law that is an acceptable practice throughout the nation

c. People who could not vote in Kentucky until 1920

d. An addition to the Constitution

e. The selection, by vote, of a candidate for office

f. To give approval

g. The fundamental law of the United States that was framed in 1787 and put into effect in 1789

h. The legislature in some states of the United States

ANSWERS: 1.d 2.f 3.g 4.h 5.b 6.e 7.a 8.c

Kentucky's Resources

Fill in the bubblegram with the names of the following Kentucky resources. Some letter clues have been provided.

- * Oil
- * Natural Gas
- * Tobacco
- * Horses
- * Cotton
- * Corvettes
- * Coal

O ◯ ___

◯ ___ T ___ ◯ ___ ___   G ◯ ___

T ___ ___ ___ ◯ ___ ◯

H ___ ___ ◯ ___ ___

C ___ ___ ◯ ◯ ___ ___ ___ ◯

___ ◯ ___ L

___ ___ ◯ T ___ ◯

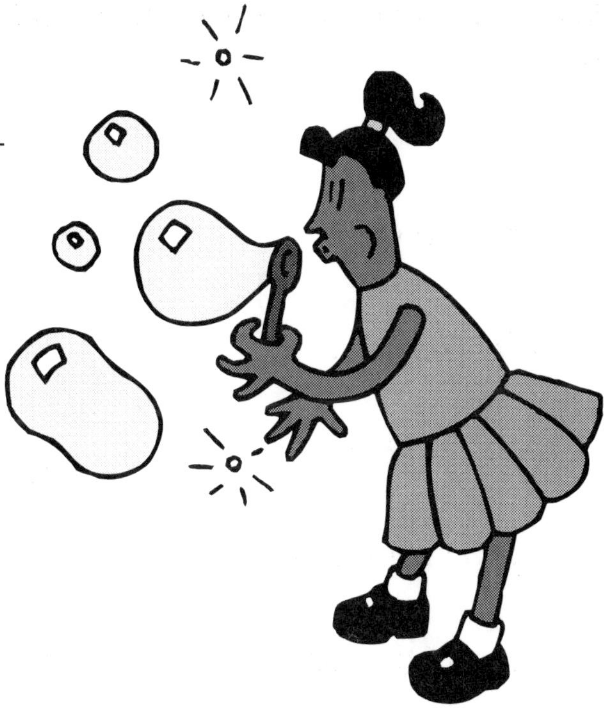

Now unscramble the "bubbled" letters to find the mystery word!
Hint: What is one way we can save our environment and natural resources?

___ ___ ___ ___ ___ ___ ___ ___ ___ ___ ___ ___

ANSWERS: oil, natural gas, tobacco, horses, tobacco, Corvettes, coal, cotton
MYSTERY WORD: conservation

Georgie's 2 Many Horses 2 Feed Day!

Count all the "2s" in the story and write your total in the box below:

Georgie was a young Lexington pioneer. He was interested in the horses his father was raising. Perhaps, he was 2 interested!

"If you want 2 help," said his father, "you can put on these 2 gloves and feed these oats 2 those 2 rows of horses."

Georgie began 2 work. He worked on 2 stalls. He finished feeding 2 horses. Then he tackled another 2 stalls, then another 2. Then Georgie decided that the sun was 2 hot, and he was 2 tired. This was not 2 much fun after all!

His friends began 2 tease him. "You are working 2 hard," they said. "We are having 2 much fun. Don't you want 2 join us?"

"My father has 2 much work 2 do," Georgie said. "But I have worked 2 hours and so I will take a 2 minute break with you."

I counted this many 2s:

ANSWER: 21

You've Got Mail!

Share the present with the past.
Send an e-mail to the past. E-mail a boy or girl from early Kentucky and tell them what they're missing in today's world.

WRITE	SAVE	SEND	DELETE	INTERNET
				NEWS AND NOTES

You may even get a message in return…a message written on parchment with a quill pen telling you what you're missing from a simpler time!

INNOVATIVE
INVENTIONS

These are just some of the amazing Kentucky inventions and inventors!

steamboat
traffic signal
aluminum foil
radio

DID YOU KNOW?
The "Happy Birthday" song was written by two sisters in Louisville!

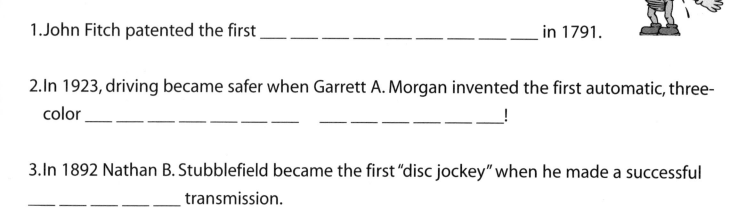

1. John Fitch patented the first ___ ___ ___ ___ ___ ___ ___ ___ ___ in 1791.

2. In 1923, driving became safer when Garrett A. Morgan invented the first automatic, three-color ___ ___ ___ ___ ___ ___ ___   ___ ___ ___ ___ ___ ___!

3. In 1892 Nathan B. Stubblefield became the first "disc jockey" when he made a successful ___ ___ ___ ___ ___ transmission.

4. If it weren't for Richard S. Reynolds' 1947 invention of ___ ___ ___ ___ ___ ___ ___ ___ ___ ___ ___ ___, we wouldn't be able to wrap a lot of our leftovers!

ANSWERS: 1. steamboat 2. traffic signal 3. radio 4. aluminum foil

Famous Kentucky People Scavenger Hunt

Here is a list of some of the famous people from our state. Go on a scavenger hunt to see if you can "capture" a fact about each person. Use an encyclopedia, almanac, or other resource you might need. Happy hunting!

FAMOUS PERSON   **FAMOUS FACT**

Budd Abbot   _____

John James Audubon   _____

Alben William Barkley   _____

Louis Dembitz Brandeis   _____

Simon B. Buckner   _____

Christopher (Kit) Carson   _____

Cassius Marcellus Clay   _____

William Clark   _____

Martha Layne Collins   _____

Jefferson Davis   _____

Casey Jones   _____

Abraham Lincoln   _____

Bill Monroe   _____

Thomas Hunt Morgan   _____

Harland ("Colonel") Sanders   _____

Nathan Stubblefield   _____

Zachary Taylor   _____

Frederick Moore Vinson   _____

Robert Penn Warren   _____

The Hatfields and the McCoys: A Legendary Feud

After the Civil War, many feuds (fights) started between families in Kentucky and other states. The most famous feud took place between the Hatfield family in West Virginia and the McCoy family in Kentucky. There are several legends as to how the feud started. One legend states that in 1878 one of the McCoys' pigs wandered over to the Hatfield farm in West Virginia. The McCoy family accused the Hatfields of shooting the pig, and a family shooting war started. For decades the two families fought, and many members of both sides were killed. Many songs and poems have been written about this family feud.

```
Q W D S Z X E R D F C V T Y M
K M E N H B G V F C D X S Z C
T F C D E S P I G F D C F V C
L K A H G F D S A A N B V C O
Y H D G U J R F W M E D R F Y
Q P E F E U D Z T I A L S K D
V M S X N C B V A L L K N V B
M J U N H Y B G T Y F R C D E
I K Z A E D V F Y H M K X S C
A E F H A T F I E L D B R M U
```

Word Pig

FEUD

HATFIELD

MCCOY

DECADES

FAMILY

PIG

Map of North America

This is a map of North America. Kentucky is one of the 50 states in North America.

Color the state of Kentucky red.

Color the rest of the United States yellow. Alaska and Hawaii are part of the United States and should also be colored yellow.

Color Canada green. Color Mexico blue.

Crazy Quilt!

Quilts made by Kentuckians have become valuable heirlooms. Heirlooms are family possessions handed down from generation to generation. Often a woman would tell a story about her family with the pattern of her quilt.

Women in the Appalachian mountains still sew quilts out of old clothes like they did a hundred years ago!

We've started this quilt just for you…now you can finish "sewing" the quilt by adding pictures that tell a story about your family. You can even use the lines below to tell a story, too!

_____

_____

_____

_____

My Old Kentucky Home...

Color the state of Kentucky. What color? Blue-green, for the Kentucky Bluegrass, of course! Then circle the capital city.

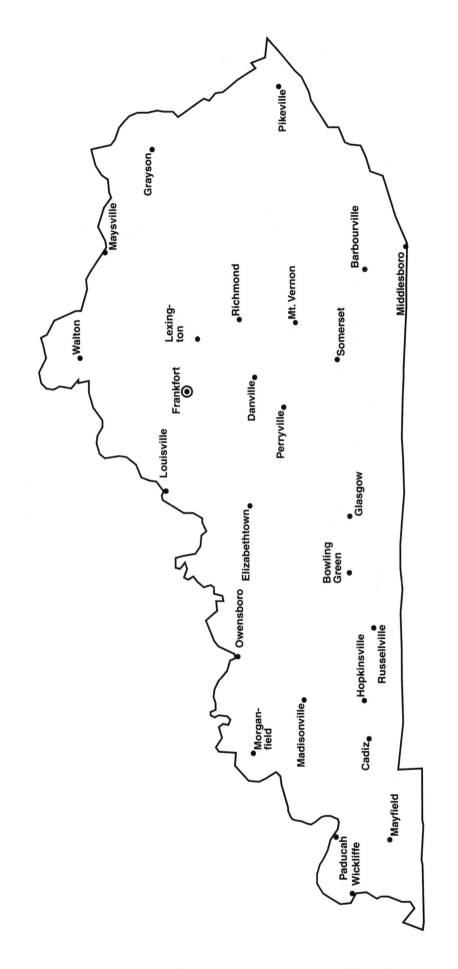

Pikeville

Grayson

Maysville

Barbourville

Walton

Richmond

Mt. Vernon

Middlesboro

Lexing-
ton

Somerset

Frankfort

Danville

Louisville

Perryville

Glasgow

Elizabethtown

Bowling
Green

Owensboro

Hopkinsville

Russellville

Morgan-
field

Madisonville

Cadiz

Mayfield

Paducah

Wickliffe

Kentucky State Greats!

How many of these State Greats from the Great State of Kentucky do you know?
Use an encyclopedia, almanac, or other resource to match the following facts with the State Great they describe.   Hint: There are 2 facts for each State Great!

_____ 1. was one half of a legendary pair who explored the West in the 1800s

_____ 2. the third largest lake in Kentucky is named for him

_____ 3. fought for women's right to vote

_____ 4. befriended the Shawnee Indians after they captured him

_____ 5. studied genetics

_____ 6. was the 16th president of the United States

_____ 7. was vice president from 1949-1953

_____ 8. the younger brother of Louisville's founder

_____ 9. ran for president three times, and lost

_____ 10. explored Kentucky and built a fort near where Lexington is located today

_____ 11. was known for his honesty

_____ 12. died the year the 19th Amendment was ratified

_____ 13. said "I had rather be right than be president"

_____ 14. won the Nobel Prize

A. Daniel Boone

B. William Clark

C. Abraham Lincoln

D. Allen B. Barkley

E. Madeline Breckenridge

F. Thomas Hunt Morgan

G. Henry Clay

ANSWERS: 1.B 2.D 3.E 4.A 5.F 6.C 7.D 8.B 9.G 10.A 11.C 12.E 13.G 14.F

Kentucky Writers

Kentucky has been the home and inspiration for many art forms. Here is a list of some of the Pulitzer prize winning and historical authors from our state.
See if you can match their names to their work. Use an encyclopedia, almanac, or other resource you might need.

1. Robert Penn Warren ____

       A. America's only three-time winner of the Pulitzer prize; *All the King's Men*

2. A.B. Guthrie, Jr. ____

       B. playwright, wrote *Teahouse of the August Moon*

3. John James Audubon ____

       C. *Clotel*; America's first African-American novelist

4. Marsha Norman ____

       D. *The Big Sky*

5. William Wells Brown ____

       E. *Birds of America*

6. John Patrick ____

       F. playwright, wrote *Getting Out*

ANSWERS: 1. A 2. D 3. E 4. F 5. C 6. B

Virtual Kentucky!

Using your knowledge of Kentucky, make a website that explains different places in Kentucky. You can even draw pictures of animals, places, people, etc., to make your very own interesting website.

Create Your Own State Quarter!

Look at the change in your pocket. You might notice that one of the coins has changed. The United States is minting new quarters, one for each of the fifty states. Each quarter has a design on it that says something special about one particular state. That means that Kentucky will have its own special quarter design.

What do you think should go on the Kentucky quarter? Draw a picture of how you would like the new Kentucky quarter to look. Make sure you include things that are special about Kentucky.

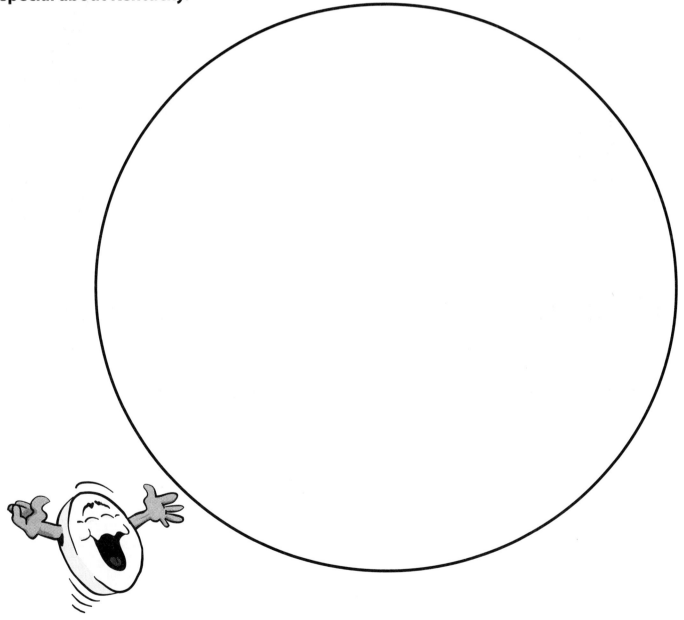

A River Runs Through It!

The state of Kentucky is blessed with many rivers, ponds, springs, and even a few swamps.
Use the chart to discover the rivers below. Come on—wade right in!

A	B	C	D	E	F	G	H	I	J	K	L	M
1	2	3	4	5	6	7	8	9	10	11	12	13
N	**O**	**P**	**Q**	**R**	**S**	**T**	**U**	**V**	**W**	**X**	**Y**	**Z**
14	15	16	17	18	19	20	21	22	23	24	25	26

1. ___ ___ ___ ___ ___ ___ ___ ___ ___
   20   5   14   14   5   19   19   5   5

2. ___ ___ ___ ___ ___ ___ ___ ___ ___ ___
   3   21   13   2   5   18   12   1   14   4

3. ___ ___ ___ ___ ___ ___ ___
   12   9   3   11   9   14   7

4. ___ ___ ___ ___ ___ ___ ___ ___
   2   9   7   19   1   14   4   25

5. ___ ___ ___ ___ ___
   7   18   5   5   14

6. ___ ___ ___ ___
   15   8   9   15

Did you know that Kentucky is in the Mississippi River Basin?

Kentucky Trivia!

The "Happy Birthday" song was written in 1893 by two sisters in Louisville, Kentucky!

All the Corvettes made by the Chevrolet Auto Company are manufactured in Bowling Green, Kentucky!

The first cheeseburger ever served was in Kaelin's Restaurant in Louisville in 1934!

The people of Pikeville drink more Pepsi-Cola per person than the people in any other city in the United States!

The American flag once had 15 stripes instead of 13. In the 1790s, Congress approved a flag that had two extra stripes – one of them for Kentucky! But in 1818 the extra stripes were taken off, and Congress decided to start adding stars for new states (instead of stripes).

In 1829, the first free-flowing oil well was created in Burkesville – by accident! When drilling a water well, people hit oil instead. It gushed over 50 feet (15 meters) into the air!

In 1832, Henry Clay asked the Senate to give two Kentuckians some land. The reason was that the men claimed that they had discovered the "secret of living forever". The Senate said, "No!"

In 1849, Kentucky passed a law saying a person couldn't hold a state office if they had ever been in a duel. Kentucky is the only state where the oath of office for the governor includes an anti-dueling requirement!

Write another fact that you know about Kentucky here:

_____

_____

Independence Day

We celebrate America's birthday on July 4. We call the 4th of July Independence Day because this is the day America declared its independence from England.

Circle the things you might enjoy on this special holiday.

Pretend you are signing the Declaration of Independence.

Write your signature here.

You can even make it fancy!

Declaration of Independence

_____

Bluegrass: Kentucky's Musical Roots

Kentucky is called the "Bluegrass State" for more than one reason. Bluegrass music is a special kind of music that came out of the mountains of eastern Kentucky. The people who settled there in the late 1700s brought traditional folk music from Scotland, Ireland, and England. Those songs became Kentucky's folk music. Bluegrass music uses instruments like guitars, fiddles, and banjos. The songs can be lively and happy, or slow and sad. Many of them tell stories of lost love or of homesickness. Bluegrass became popular all over America in the 1940s when William Smith "Bill" Monroe began playing it on his radio show. There are bluegrass festivals every year in Kentucky, and thousands of people go to hear this traditional music.

Use these facts and the Word Bank to complete the bubblegram.

1. Kentucky's traditional music is called ◯ __ __ __ __ __ __ __ __.

2. This kind of music uses instruments like the __ __ __ __ __ ◯ and the __ __ ◯ __ ◯.

3. Kentucky settlers brought __ ◯ ◯ __ music with them from Ireland, Scotland, and England.

4. This kind of music started in the ◯ __ __ __ __ ◯ __ __ of eastern Kentucky.

5. You can go to different __ ◯ __ __ __ __ ◯ __ in Kentucky to hear this music.

Now unscramble the "bubble" letters to find out the secret words!

(Hint: Who first made bluegrass music famous?)

__ __ __ __   __ __ __ __ __ __

WORD BANK

MOUNTAINS
BLUEGRASS
FESTIVALS
GUITAR
BANJO
FOLK

MYSTERY WORDS: BILL MONROE

ANSWERS: 1. BLUEGRASS 2. GUITAR, BANJO 3. FOLK 4. MOUNTAINS 5. FESTIVALS

Kentucky Gazetteer

A gazetteer is a list of places. Use the word bank to complete the names of some of these famous places in our state:

1. My Old Kentucky Home State Park in _B_ __ __ __ __ __ __ __ _N_

2. The Kentucky Derby at _C_ __ __ __ __ __ __ __ _L_ Downs

3. _L_ __ __ __ __ __ _Y_ Hall in Frankfort

4. Daniel _B_ __ __ __ _E_ National Forest

5. _M_ __ __ __ __ __ _H_ Cave, near Bowling Green

6. Fort _K_ __ __ _X_ , near Louisville

7. Kentucky _H_ __ __ __ _E_ Park in Lexington

8. _C_ __ __ __ __ __ __ __ __ _D_ Gap National Historical Park

9. _S_ __ __ __ __ _R_ Village near Harrodsburg

10. _P_ __ __ __ __ __ __ __ __ __ _E_ Battlefield

WORD BANK

Churchill	Mammoth
Horse	Shaker
Knox	Boone
Liberty	Bardstown
Cumberland	Perryville

State Stuff Jumble

Arrange the jumbled letters in the proper order for the names of Kentucky's state symbols.

CARDINAL   **GOLDENROD**   **KENTUCKY BASS**

FRESHWATER PEARL **TULIP TREE**   **GRAY SQUIRREL**

BRACHIOPOD   **VICEROY**

1. DGORELNOD _____ (state flower)

2. LIPTU ERET _____ (state tree)

3. DOPBICRAHO _____ (state fossil)

4. YORCVIE _____ (state butterfly)

5. KYUKENTC SABS _____ (state fish)

6. RAYG RERIQULS _____ (state wild animal)

7. RAWTERSFHE RALEP _____ (state gemstone)

8. RACIDNLA _____ (state bird)

Kentucky Towns Word Wheel!

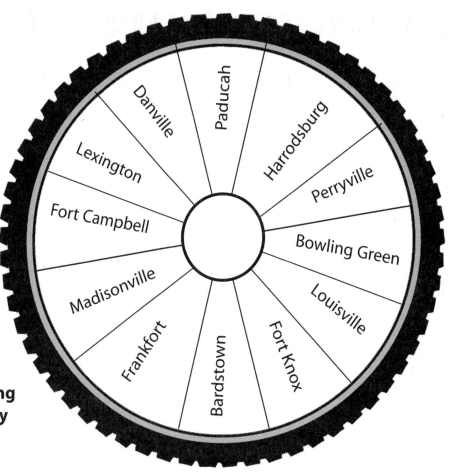

Using the Word Wheel of Kentucky names, answer the following questions about Kentucky towns.

1. The 101st Airborne Division is stationed at _____.

2. The Kentucky Derby is held every year in _____ .

3. Stephen Foster was inspired to write "My Old Kentucky Home" in _____.

4. Kentucky's bloodiest Civil War battle was fought in _____.

5. Kentucky's capital is located in _____.

6. You will find the University of Kentucky in _____.

7. The United States gold reserve can be found at _____.

8. The oldest town in Kentucky is _____.

9. Kentucky's first state constitution was framed in _____.

10. _____ was founded by William Clark (of Lewis and Clark fame).

ANSWERS: 1. Fort Campbell 2. Louisville 3. Bardstown 4. Perryville 5. Frankfort 6. Lexington 7. Fort Knox 8. Harrodsburg 9. Danville 10. Paducah

Pioneer Corn Husk Doll

You can make a corn husk doll similar to the dolls Kentucky settlers' children might have played with! Here's how:

You will need:
- corn husks (or strips of cloth)
- string
- scissors

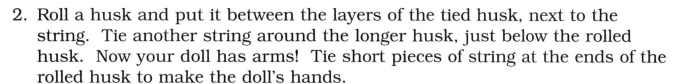

1. Select a long piece of corn husk and fold it in half. Tie a string about one inch down from the fold to make the doll's head.

2. Roll a husk and put it between the layers of the tied husk, next to the string. Tie another string around the longer husk, just below the rolled husk. Now your doll has arms! Tie short pieces of string at the ends of the rolled husk to make the doll's hands.

3. Make your doll's waist by tying another string around the longer husk.

4. If you want your doll to have legs, cut the longe husk up the middle. Tie the two halves at the bottom to make feet.

5. Add eyes and a nose to your doll with a marker. You could use corn silk for the doll's hair.

Now you can make a whole family of dolls!

Timeline

A timeline is a list of important events and the year that they happened. You can use a timeline to understand more about history. Read the timeline about Kentucky history, then see if you can answer the questions at the bottom.

1774..........Kentucky's first permanent town is founded; they call it Harrodstown

1778..........George Rogers Clark defeats the British at Kaskaskia, Cahokia, and Vincennes

1782..........The Battle of Blue Licks (Kentucky's last battle of the American Revolution)

1792..........Kentucky frames its first Constitution and becomes the 15th state

1848..........The largest slave uprising in U.S. history happens near Lexington when 55 slaves try to escape

1861...........Kentucky's legislature declares its neutrality in the Civil War

1906...........The Black Patch War begins

1929...........The stock market crashes and the Great Depression begins

1962...........The state legislature passes laws to regulate strip mining

1966...........The Kentucky Civil Rights Act is passed

Choose the correct year to complete each statement.

1. If you had heard about an American victory at Cahokia, the year would be _____.

2. If you were a settler looking for a new community, the year would be _____.

3. If you were excited to learn that the area where you live in had become a state, the year would be _____.

4. If you learned that the restaurants and schools weren't segregated anymore, the year might be _____.

5. If you were a slave who wanted to try to escape from Lexington, the year might be _____.

Kentucky Banks

Kentucky banks provide essential financial services.
Some of the services that banks provide include:

- They lend money to consumers to purchase goods and service such as houses, cars, and education.
- They lend money to producers who start new businesses.
- They issue credit cards.
- They provide savings accounts and pay interest to savers.
- They provide checking accounts.

Check whether you would have more, less, or the same amount of money after each event.

1. You deposit your paycheck into your checking account.   MORE   LESS   SAME

2. You put $1,000 in your savings account.   MORE   LESS   SAME

3. You use your credit card to buy new school clothes.   MORE   LESS   SAME

4. You borrow money from the bank to open a toy store.   MORE   LESS   SAME

5. You write a check at the grocery store.   MORE   LESS   SAME

6. You transfer money from checking to savings.   MORE   LESS   SAME

7. You withdraw money to buy pizza.   MORE   LESS   SAME

8. You deposit the pennies from your piggy bank.   MORE   LESS   SAME

9. You see the interest in your savings account.   MORE   LESS   SAME

10. You use the ATM machine to get money to buy a book.   MORE   LESS   SAME

ANSWERS: 1.MORE 2. MORE 3. SAME 4. MORE 5. LESS 6. SAME 7.LESS 8.MORE 9.MORE 10.LESS

Kentucky Celebrity Bubblegram

Many famous people have lived in Kentucky.
Complete the bubblegram using the clues below.

1. The 16th president of the United States, Abraham __ ◯ __ __ __ ◯

2. The long hunter who founded Boonesborough, Daniel __ __ __ __ ◯

3. The author of *Uncle Tom's Cabin*, Harriet Beecher __ ◯ __ ◯ ◯

4. The famous painter of birds, John James __ __ ◯ ◯ __ __ ◯

5. The 12th president of the United States, Zachary ◯ __ __ __ __ __

6. The vocal abolitionist, __ ◯ __ __ __ __ ◯ Marcellus Clay

7. The leader of the Confederate states during the Civil War, Jefferson ◯ __ __ __ __

Now unscramble the "bubbled" letters to complete Kentucky's state motto:

__ __ __ __ __ __ __ __ __ __ __ __ __, DIVIDED WE FALL

WORD BANK

CASSIUS	BOONE
AUDUBON	DAVIS
STOWE	TAYLOR
LINCOLN	

The Black Patch War

Tobacco has always been an important crop in Kentucky. In the early 1900s, a group of tobacco companies decided they wanted to buy all of the state's tobacco for themselves. That way, they would not have to compete with anyone and could buy tobacco for very low prices. This hurt the tobacco farmers, and many of them refused to sell their tobacco to the companies. Other farmers continued to sell their tobacco to the companies. In 1906, these two groups of farmers started fighting. That was the beginning of the Black Patch War, which lasted until 1909. Many people were hurt during the Black Patch War, but when it ended tobacco farmers were able to sell their tobacco for a fairer price.

Pretend you are a tobacco farmer in 1906. Write a letter to the governor telling him about your unhappiness with the tobacco companies.

_____

_____

_____

_____

_____

_____

_____

_____

_____

_____

Women in Kentucky's History

Kentucky has been the home of many brave and influential women. Here is a list of some of these famous females. See if you can match the facts to these women's names. Use an encyclopedia, almanac, or any resource you might need.

1. Jenny Wiley

2. Laura Clay

3. Sophonisba Preston Breckinridge

4. Martha Layne Collins

5. Delia Ann Webster

6. Catherine Spalding

7. Margaret Ingels

8. Catherine M. Nation

A. first woman lawyer in Kentucky

B. first female governor of Kentucky

C. captured by Indians in 1789, escaped in 1800

D. leader in the temperance movement during the early 1900s

E. first woman in the United States to earn a Ph.D. in mechanical engineering

F. abolitionist who went to jail for helping 3 slaves to escape in 1844

G. founded the Roman Catholic Sisters of Charity of Nazareth

H. daughter of Cassius Marcellus Clay, president of KERA for 24 years

ANSWERS: 1.C 2.H 3.A 4.B 5.F 6.G 7.E 8.D

It's Money in the Bank!

You spent the summer working at your uncle's manufacturing plant in Lexington and you made a lot of money...$500 to be exact!
Find the answers to the following money problems.

TOTAL EARNED: $500.00

I will pay back my Mom this much
for money I borrowed when I first
started working (Thanks Mom!):   A. $20.00

     Subtract A ($20.00) from $500   B. _____

I will give my little brother this much
money for taking my phone messages
while I was at work: C. $10.00

     Subtract C ($10.00) from B   D. _____

I will spend this much on a special
treat or reward for myself: E. $25.00

     Subtract E ($25.00) from D   F. _____

I will save this much for college: G. $300.00

     Subtract G ($300.00) from F   H. _____

I will put this much in my new
savings account so I can buy school
clothes: I. $100.00

     Subtract I ($100.00) from H   J. _____

     TOTAL STILL AVAILABLE
     (use answer J)   _____

     TOTAL SPENT
     (add A, C, and E)   _____

Good Golly! Kentucky Geography Word Search

Kentucky has lots and lots of cities and towns spread all around.

See if you can find these Kentucky cities in the Word Search below!

Louisville   Murray   Owensboro   Paducah
Perryville   Pikeville   Ashland   Lexington
Bowling Green   Frankfort   Harrodsburg
Hopkinsville

```
F  R  A  N  K  F  O  R  T  P  L  W  X  N  W  T  I  C
P  L  O  K  I  J  U  H  L  O  U  I  S  V  I  L  L  E
E  C  X  N  C  H  A  Q  F  G  J  M  U  R  R  A  Y  B
R  K  B  I  N  X  P  L  Z  V  P  L  K  X  H  C  G  A
R  H  O  P  K  I  N  S  V  I  L  L  E  V  A  L  L  S
Y  P  L  X  M  W  A  S  Z  A  E  I  K  O  R  Q  E  H
V  F  P  V  K  K  L  M  F  B  G  N  H  N  R  J  X  L
I  X  B  Q  A  I  C  L  Q  S  C  F  G  K  O  N  I  A
L  Q  B  O  W  L  I  N  G  G  R  E  E  N  D  F  N  N
L  P  M  G  A  C  D  V  T  S  J  B  M  G  S  H  G  D
E  P  Q  Y  R  G  S  C  W  X  L  S  N  V  B  X  T  A
M  B  K  B  P  A  D  U  C  A  H  Q  D  F  U  P  O  W
A  G  Y  P  O  E  F  Q  A  W  S  V  B  C  R  F  N  P
V  C  L  R  O  W  E  N  S  B  O  R  O  Q  G  X  J  D
A  E  C  H  V  A  C  D  E  P  I  K  E  V  I  L  L  E
```

How Many People in Kentucky?

STATE OF KENTUCKY
CENSUS REPORT

Every ten years, it's time for Kentuckians to stand up and be counted. Since 1790, the United States has conducted a census, or count, of each of its citizens. Practice filling out a pretend census form.

Name _____ Age [ ]

Place of Birth _____

Current Address _____

Does your family own or rent where you live? _____

How long have you lived in Kentucky? _____

How many people are in your family? _____

How many females? [ ]   How many males? [ ]

What are their ages? _____

How many rooms are in your house? [ ]

How is your home heated? _____

How many cars does your family own? [ ]

How many telephones in your home? [ ]

Is your home a farm? _____

Sounds pretty nosy, doesn't it? But a census is very important. The information is used for all kinds of purposes, including setting budgets, zoning land, determining how many schools to build, and much more. The census helps Kentucky leaders plan for the future needs of its citizens. Hey, that's you!!

Kentucky Cities

Circle Frankfort in red. It is our state's capital. The star is the map symbol for our capital.

Circle Louisville in yellow. It is the largest city in Kentucky.

Circle Lexington in blue. It is Kentucky's 2nd largest city, and home of the University of Kentucky Wildcats.

Circle Ashland in brown. You can find Woodland Indian burial grounds from 800 B.C. in its Central Park!

Circle Owensboro in orange. It is the home of the International Bar-B-Q Festival.

Add your city or town to the map if it's not here. Circle it in green. Give it a ☺ symbol to show you live there.

Oops! The compass rose is missing its cardinal directions. Write N, S, E, W, on the compass rose.

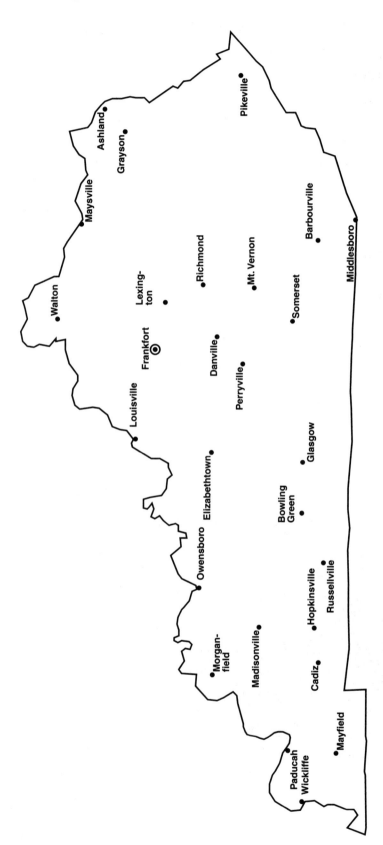

Endangered!

Each state has a list of the endangered species in their state. An animal is labeled endangered when it is in danger of becoming extinct. Land development, changes in climate and weather, and changes in the number of predators are all factors that can cause an animal to become extinct. Kentucky is full of wildlife. If you went out in the woods, you might see deer, foxes, mink, opposums, raccoons, and woodchucks. Unfortunately, some animals have become endangered species. Today many states are passing laws to help save animals on the endangered species list.

Unscramble the names of the endangered animals in Kentucky below:

LBAKC RAEB _____

PMAWS BIBRAT _____

VRIER TOTRE _____

RACUOG _____

Kentucky's State Song

In 1852, Stephen Foster visited his cousin's home in Bardstown, Kentucky. According to legend, Foster wrote the song *My Old Kentucky Home* to capture the beauty of that place and the emotions he felt there. In 1928, the state legislature chose *My Old Kentucky Home* to be Kentucky's state song. Kentuckians have been known to weep when they hear this song! You can still visit the house that inspired this beautiful melody at the My Old Kentucky Home State Park in Bardstown.

Here is the first verse of *My Old Kentucky Home*.

"The sun shines bright in the old Kentucky home
'tis summer, the people are gay,
the corn top's ripe and the meadow's in bloom
while the birds make music all the day.
The young folks roll on the little cabin floor
all merry, all happy, and bright.
By'n by hard times comes a-knocking at the door,
then my old Kentucky home, good night."

**Write your own second verse
about Kentucky.**

_____

_____

_____

_____

_____

_____

Getting Ready To Vote

When you turn 18, you will be eligible to vote. Your vote counts! Many elections have been won by just a few votes. The following is a form for your personal voting information. You will need to be a good research student to get all the answers!

I will be eligible to vote on this date _____

I live in this Congressional District _____

I live in this State Senate District _____

I live in this State Representative District _____

I live in this Voting Precinct _____

The first local election I can vote in will be _____

The first state election I can vote in will be _____

The first national election I can vote in will be _____

The governor of our state is _____

One of my state senators is _____

One of my state representatives is _____

The local public office I would like to run for is _____

The state public office I would like to run for is _____

The federal public office I would like to run for is _____

Kentucky State Seal

The Kentucky state seal was adopted in 1792 (the year it became a state). It shows a pioneer and a diplomat greeting each other with a friendly embrace.

Color the state seal.

Animal Scramble

Unscramble the names of these animals you might find in your Kentucky backyard.

Write the answers in the word wheel below the picture of each animal.

1. *kipchnum*   Hint: She can store more than a hundred seeds in her cheeks!

2. *ethiw dleait ered*   Hint: He raises the underside of his tail to signal danger!

3. *nrocoac*   Hint: He has very sensitive "fingers" and uses them to find food.

4. *ntseare ttoncoliat bitbra*   Hint: She would love to eat the cabbages in your garden!

5. *yarg lquiersr*   Hint: He scurries around all day, burying and digging up acorns!

A Quilt of Many Counties

Kentucky has 120 counties. To make a "quilt" of your state, use different colored markers or crayons to shade in the counties. Write in the name of your county, town, and your state's capital.

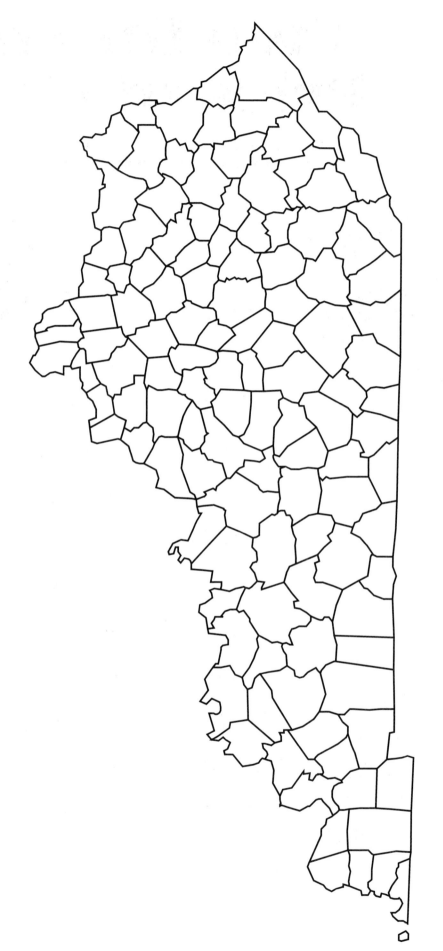

Two for the Price of One!

How many of these two-name places can you match? You might need a map or an atlas to help you figure them out.

1. Honey
2. Blue
3. Monkey's
4. Morning
5. Rabbit
6. Bowling
7. Black
8. Roaring
9. Fort
10. Eighty
11. Sassafras
12. Stamping

A. Knox
B. Hash
C. Diamond
D. Green
E. Eight
F. Eyebrow
G. Ground
H. Gnat
I. Bee
J. Spring
K. View
L. Ridge

ANSWERS: 1. I 2. C 3. F 4. K 5. B 6. D 7. H 8. J 9. A 10. E 11. L 12. G

Major Minorities

Dr. Martin Luther King, Jr. was one of the most famous civil rights leaders. He wanted all Americans to live freely anywhere, and not just in segregated neighborhoods. Dr. King had a dream. His dream was equal rights for all Americans. He worked very hard to make all Americans "free at last."

Many other African-Americans and Hispanic-Americans made significant contributions to the state of Kentucky, the nation, and in some cases, the world. Below are a few.

Try matching the people with their accomplishments.

_____ 1. Whitney M. Young, Jr.

_____ 2. Georgia Powers

_____ 3. Moneta J. Sleet, Jr.

_____ 4. Mae Jemison

_____ 5. William Wells Brown

_____ 6. James Farmer

_____ 7. Barbara C. Jordan

_____ 8. Andrew "Rube" Foster

A. civil rights leader and director of the National Urban League from 1961-1971

B. first African-American novelist

C. first African-American woman in space

D. founded Congress Of Racial Equality

E. Kentucky's first female African-American state senator

F. Hispanic leader; served as cabinet member for President Clinton

G. first African-American woman from the south to serve in the U.S. Congress

H. first African-American to win the Pulitzer Prize in photography

ANSWERS: 1.A 2.E 3.F 4.C 5.B 6.D 7.G 8.H

Let's Have Words!

Make as many words as you can from the letters in the words

United We Stand, Divided We Fall!

_____   _____   _____

_____   _____   _____

_____   _____   _____

_____   _____   _____

_____   _____   _____

_____   _____   _____

_____   _____   _____

_____   _____   _____

_____   _____   _____

_____   _____   _____

One State, Many Nations

When the first Europeans came to Kentucky, it was an enormous hunting ground. Five Native American nations were settled around this land, but there were no permanent Native American settlements. These nations agreed not to live on the hunting ground, but to share it for food. Find the names of these Native American nations in the word search below:

Word Bank

CHEROKEE   CHICKASAW

WYANDOT

DELAWARE   SHAWNEE

```
C  V  A  E  C  K  O  H  S  W  Z  I
H  X  B  I  K  H  D  Z  A  Y  L  K
I  G  C  K  D  O  H  V  Q  A  V  A
C  N  J  W  Y  F  C  K  Q  N  V  X
K  C  H  E  R  O  K  E  E  D  G  D
A  E  Z  A  M  O  C  D  R  O  S  L
S  F  O  M  Y  N  O  L  M  T  D  E
A  K  D  D  M  S  H  A  W  N  E  E
W  D  E  L  A  W  A  R  E  X  K  L
```

Which Founding Person Am I?

From the Word Bank, find my name and fill in the blank.

WORD BANK

Thomas Walker   George Washington
John Finley   Abraham Lincoln
James Harrod   Daniel Boone
Jefferson Davis   Lewis Clark

1. I was a doctor from Virginia who loved to explore new lands. In 1750, I ventured into Kentucky and discovered the Cumberland Gap.
   WHO AM I? _____

2. I followed the Ohio River to the location near today's Louisville in 1752. I am credited with founding Kentucky.
   WHO AM I? _____

3. I was born in a log cabin in Hodgenville in 1809. I became the 16th president in 1860.
   WHO AM I? _____

4. I founded the first permanent European settlement in Kentucky in 1774. I even named the town after myself!
   WHO AM I? _____

5. I led a group of settlers along the Wilderness Trail in 1775. Together we founded the town of Boonesborough.
   WHO AM I? _____

6. I was the first President of the United States. Some people call me the "Father of Our Country."
   WHO AM I? _____

7. I was born only 100 miles away from Abraham Lincoln's birthplace. I was the leader of the Confederate States during the Civil War.
   WHO AM I? _____

8. I was a banker who loved thoroughbred horses. I built Churchill Downs in 1875, and started the Kentucky Derby.
   WHO AM I? _____

ANSWERS: 1. Thomas Walker 2. James Finley 3. Abraham Lincoln 4. James Harrod 5. Daniel Boone 6. George Washington 7. Jefferson Davis 8. Lewis Clark

It Could Happen - and It Did!

These historical events from Kentucky's past are all out of sequence.

Can you put them back together in the correct order?
(There's a great big hint at the end of each sentence.)

–The first Kentucky Derby race was run (1875)
–The Kentucky Civil Rights Act was passed (1966)
–James Harrod founded the first permanent European settlement in Kentucky (1774)
–The Civil War began (1861)
–Thomas Walker explored the Cumberland Gap (1750)
–Kentucky became the 15th state (1792)
–The Black Patch War began in western Kentucky (1906)
–The United States government started storing gold at Fort Knox (1936)
–Abraham Lincoln was elected the 16th president (1860)
–The Hatfields and the McCoys began a bloody feud (1878)

1. _____

2. _____

3. _____

4. _____

5. _____

6. _____

7. _____

8. _____

9. _____

10. _____

Make A Shawnee Indian Vest

Many Native Americans wore clothing that was made from the skins of deer. To make your deer skin vest, you will need a brown paper bag. Lay the bag flat, as shown in the picture. Cut out holes for your arms and neck. Make a long slit in one side of the bag.

Ideas for decorating your vest:

- glue buttons, glitter, and feathers on the vest

- use markers or crayons to draw Native American symbols on the vest

- make fringe at the bottom of the bag by snipping along the edges of the bag

- decorate your vest with beads, shells, etc.

Get together with your friends and have a great "pow-wow"!

Move to the Big City

You have lived on a farm in a small Kentucky town all your life. Your family has made the decision to move to a big city. What will you do? Where will you live? How will you get around? Write a letter to your friend in Louisville and ask her all of these questions. This is what she writes back to you:

Similar Symbols

Kentucky has many symbols including a state bird, tree, flower, and flag.
Circle the item in each row that is not a symbol of Kentucky.

A Split Decision

Did you know that Kentucky didn't choose sides during the Civil War? When many other states had joined either the Union or the Confederacy, the Kentucky government declared that it was neutral when the war started. Both the Union and the Confederacy had a star for Kentucky in their flags! About 35,000 Kentucky men fought for the South, and 75,000 men fought for the North. What's more, the leaders of *both* the Union and the Confederacy were native Kentuckians! The president of the Confederate states, Jefferson Davis, was born only 100 miles (161 kilometers) from where Abraham Lincoln was born! Kentucky was definitely divided during the Civil War!

Use these facts to complete the bubblegram.

1. About 35,000 Kentucky men fought for the _____.
2. Abraham _____ was president of the Union.
3. The president of the Confederate states was Jefferson _____.
4. Both the North and the South had a star for _____ in their flags.
5. About 75,000 Kentucky men fought for the _____.

1. __ __ __ ◯ __

2. ◯ __ __ __ __ __ __

3. __ ◯ __ __ __

4. __ ◯ __ ◯ __ __ __

5. ◯ __ ◯ __ __

Now unscramble the "bubble" letters to find out the mystery word!
(Hint: it describes what Kentucky was during the Civil War)

__ __ __ __ __ __ __

Water, Water, Everywhere

There are no large natural lakes in Kentucky, but there are several man-made lakes. These lakes were created by building huge dams on several rivers in Kentucky. **Find the names of these artificial lakes in the word search below.**

Word Bank

BARKLEY

KENTUCKY CUMBERLAND

BUCKHORN NOLIN CARR FORK

```
B  S  W  F  B  T  X  B  K  D  C
U  B  X  D  F  W  G  D  E  L  F
C  B  A  R  K  L  E  Y  N  S  X
K  H  U  P  O  W  M  X  T  N  V
H  G  X  N  S  Z  Y  Q  U  Z  M
O  G  V  N  P  C  L  R  C  G  T
R  N  O  L  I  N  W  S  K  D  W
N  O  X  V  Z  W  B  V  Y  G  E
H  C  A  R  R  F  O  R  K  O  S
C  U  M  B  E  R  L  A  N  D  O
```

Know your Kentucky Facts!

Pop quiz! It's time to test your knowledge of Kentucky! Try to answer all of the questions before you look at the answers.

1. Daniel Boone founded Boonesborough in:
   ○ a) 1775
   ○ b) 1675
   ○ c) 1975

2. Kentucky is both a state and a:
   ○ a) nation
   ○ b) county
   ○ c) commonwealth

3. The first permanent European settlement in Kentucky was founded by:
   ○ a) Daniel Boone
   ○ b) La Salle
   ○ c) James Harrod

4. Kentucky became the 15th state of the Union in:
   ○ a) 1792
   ○ b) 1776
   ○ c) 1769

5. Kentucky's capital is:
   ○ a) Louisville
   ○ b) Frankfort
   ○ c) Lexington

6. At Churchill Downs you can watch the
   ○ a) Kentucky Bluegrass Festival
   ○ b) re-enactment of the Battle of Perryville
   ○ c) Kentucky Derby

7. During the Civil War, Kentucky was part of the:
   ○ a) Union
   ○ b) Confederate states
   ○ c) neither, Kentucky was neutral

8. Kentucky's most important mineral is:
   ○ a) diamond
   ○ b) granite
   ○ c) coal

9. You can go to My Old Kentucky Home State Park to learn about the state:
   ○ a) song
   ○ b) animal
   ○ c) bird

10. The Black Patch War was over:
   ○ a) coal
   ○ b) tobacco
   ○ c) slavery

ANSWERS: 1.a 2.c 3.c 4.a 5.b 6.c 7.c 8.c 9.a 10.b

Scavenger Hunt Kentucky Style

This is a fun hunt that includes your friends or classmates. Read the list below, find someone who has "been there and done that," get their signature and move on to the next item on your list. See how fast you can complete the scavenger hunt. Have your teacher, or parent, check the answers to Part 2.

Part 1
Find someone who has:

- been to the state capitol building _____
- seen the Kentucky Derby _____
- met a bluegrass musician _____
- visited Fort Knox _____
- attended the Kentucky State Fair _____
- been to a Kentucky Wildcats game _____

Part 2
Find someone who can:

- name Kentucky's statehood date _____
- say the state motto _____
- name the state capital _____
- tell who James Finley was _____
- name a major Kentucky river _____
- name the governor of Kentucky _____
- name the state tree _____

Kentucky Spelling Bee

Good spelling is a good habit. Study the words on the left side of the page. Then fold the page in half and "take a spelling test" on the right side. Have a buddy read the words aloud to you. When done, unfold the page and check your spelling. Keep your score. GOOD LUCK.

Cumberland

brachiopod

pioneer

tobacco

industry

bluegrass

Frankfort

Churchill

mammoth

thoroughbred

goldenrod

viceroy

assembly

neutral

Reconstruction

1._____

2._____

3._____

4._____

5._____

6._____

7._____

8._____

9._____

10._____

11._____

12._____

13._____

14._____

15._____

Each of the 15 items is worth 5 points. 75 is a perfect score. How many did you get right?

Bio Bottles

Biography bottles are 2 or 3 liter bottles, emptied and cleaned. They are then decorated like your favorite Kentucky character. They can represent someone from the past or the present. Use your imagination!

**Here are some items
you may want to use to help you:**

2 or 3 liter bottles

scissors

glue

felt

balloon or styrofoam ball for head

paint

yarn for hair

fabric for clothes

A Tasty Treat: Derby Pie

Celebrate the Kentucky Derby with this tasty treat! This simple and gooey recipe is guaranteed to please. Just don't try to run any races after eating a few pieces!

Ingredients you will need:

1/4 pound (one stick) of butter, melted
1 cup sugar
2 eggs, slightly beaten
1 teaspoon vanilla extract
1/2 cup all-purpose flour
2/3 cup chopped pecans
3/4 cup chocolate chips
9-inch pie crust

Directions:

Preheat the oven to 350° F.
Mix all the ingredients together
and pour into the pie crust.
Bake for 40-45 minutes.
Enjoy!

Tracing Daniel Boone

In the 1700s, Kentucky was explored by many "long hunters." The famous Daniel Boone was one of these hunters. In 1767, he first went to Kentucky to hunt. In 1769, Boone followed the Warrior's Path, and found the fertile Bluegrass Region. He blazed a trail called "Boone's Trace" through the great Cumberland Gap in 1774. He even built a fort and named it after himself! In 1775, he founded Boonesborough on the Kentucky River, just south of today's Lexington. Daniel Boone was certainly a busy hunter and trail blazer!

Help Daniel Boone blaze his trail through Kentucky!

Painted Turtle

Painted turtles live in waterways all across North America. They can grow 10 inches long.

"Paint" this turtle using the color key.

COLOR KEY

R = red   B = blue
Y = yellow   G = green

How many spots are on this turtle? _____

ANSWER: 29

Screaming Eagles!

Kentucky is the home of the 101st Airborne Division (the "Screaming Eagles") of the United States Army. The Screaming Eagles are based at Fort Campbell, which is located near Hopkinsville, Kentucky. This army base was built in 1942 and named after Brigadier General William Bowen Campbell. Back then it was called Camp Campbell, and was originally built to hold 23,000 soldiers. Many soldiers were trained there to fight in World War II. It was renamed Fort Campbell in 1950, and in 1956 the 101st Airborne made it their home. Now Fort Campbell is one of the largest army bases in the country. Thousands of soldiers work, train, and live there.

Fill in the bubblegram by using the clues below.

1. The 101st _____ Division can be found at Fort Campbell.
2. Fort Campbell was founded in nineteen-___-two.
3. Fort _____ is near Hopkinsville, Kentucky.
4. Fort Campbell was named after Brigadier General William _____ Campbell.
5. The 101st is also called the "Screaming _____."

1. __ __ __ __ __ __ __ ◯

2. __ __ ◯ __ __

3. __ ◯ __ __ __ __ __ ◯

4. __ __ __ ◯ __

5. __ __ ◯ __ ◯ __

Now unscrambled the "bubble" letters to discover the mystery word.
(Hint: What is the rank of the commander of Fort Campbell?)

__ __ __ __ __ __ __

How Big is Our State?

Our state is the 37th largest state in the U.S. It is made up of 40,411 square miles (104,664 square kilometers).

Can you answer the following questions?

1. How many states are there in the United States?

   _____

2. This many states are smaller than our state:

   _____

3. This many states are larger than our state:

   _____

4. One mile = 5,280 _____ _____ _____ _____

   HINT:

5. Use a map scale to determine the distance between your hometown and Washington, D.C.
   Write the distance here: _____

Spelunk!
Kentucky's Caves

Did you know that parts of Kentucky are hollow? Kentucky is the home of Mammoth Cave, the world's longest cave system. There are 348 miles (540 kilometers) of underground passages to explore in Mammoth Cave. At Mammoth Cave National Park, you can follow guides through underground lakes, rivers, and even waterfalls! You can also learn how to "spelunk" (investigate caves). Be careful not to fall in the Bottomless Pit!

Help the spelunker find his way out of the cave tunnels.

FINISH

"K" Is For Kentucky

K is for the Kentucky Derby.

E is for eating "burgoo."

N is for neutrality during the Civil War.

T is for thoroughbred horses.

U is for United We Stand, Divided We Fall.

C is for the cardinal, our state bird.

K is for Kentucky bluegrass music.

Y is for YOU, Kentucky's future!